TOO MUCH SALT AND PEPPER

TOO MUCH SALT AND PEPPER

Two Porcupines with Prickly Spines
Who Make You Laugh and *Think*

by

SAM CAMPBELL
The Philosopher of the Forest

Cover illustration by Lars Justinen

Inside illustrations by Will Forrest

A B Publishing, Inc.
Ithaca, Michigan
www.abpub.com

Cover Artist:
James Converse

Cover Designer:
Chrystique Neibauer

TOO MUCH SALT AND PEPPER by Sam Campbell, illustrated by Will Forrest. Copyright 1944 by Simon & Schuster, Inc. Copyright renewed © 1972 by Mrs. Virginia Campbell Kerry. Reprinted by arrangement with Simon & Schuster Books for Young Readers, an imprint of Simon & Schuster Children's Publishing Division. All rights reserved.

Printed in the United States of America

Published by:
A. B. Publishing, Inc.
Ithaca, MI 48847
www.abpub.com

CONTENTS

CONTENTS

IX

TOO MUCH SALT AND PEPPER

I

A HIGHLY SEASONED WELCOME

LATE one May day when the magic of approaching evening was spreading over the north country, there was regal ceremony afoot in our forest Sanctuary. Even a stranger to the region would have discerned as much had he looked or listened to the fuss and flurry which were taking place. The very air seemed to quiver with beauty and merriment. The sun was already in the afternoon sky, high lighting mountainous clouds which hung immobile at the horizon. And all the far-flung beauty of the heavens lived again in the mirrored lake.

An old crow hurried across the brilliant sky. Maybe to some his cry would have sounded like the familiar *caw, caw, caw;* but to us who stood under spell of the moment, it seemed he said, "Awake! Awake! All you children of the forest, the party has begun." A belted kingfisher, perched on a barren bough, caught the spirit of the moment and playfully dived into the shallow water at the shore, uttering his raucous laughter as he rose on wing again.

It was all wonderful to see! Graceful birches and sturdy oaks primped in the gathering evening light, proudly displaying their tresses of new-born leaves.

Tiny star flowers and dainty violets strutted and posed their prettiest on the woodland carpet. Pine trees stood still and straight to add dignity to the scene. Juneberry blossoms flung their white beauty against the flaming color of the sky.

"Awake! Awake! They have returned—the party has begun!" cawed the old crow, and the sky became dotted with many of his kind echoing his call.

Surely something of importance and great joy was happening! An olive-backed thrush wove his song into the stillness. High in the brilliant heavens an eagle circled in effortless flight, gaining for himself a superior view of the festivities. An enormous old heron glided into a little bay and settled among the reeds, steadied himself on one stiltlike leg, and stood as if he had suddenly turned to stone. A chipmunk raced to a vantage point on an old stump, and a red squirrel perched on the limb of a wild cherry tree, chattering loudly as if by his voice he could rivet the wilderness together.

Giny and I stood at the shore of this little forest lake looking upon this elaborate ceremony. Giny is Mrs. Sam Campbell. In her heart glows a love for the living and growing things of nature. Our canoe, loaded with luggage, floated where wavelets broke against the shore. Now we were ready to begin the last leg of our journey back to the Sanctuary—our home.

"The woods people need not have done all this just because we were coming home," said Giny, referring to the carnival loveliness about us. "It is nice of them, but something simpler would have been sufficient—just to tell us we are welcome."

But the wild world only became more beautiful, and laughed at her call for moderation. Nature deals in extravagance. Sunset hues deepened to old gold, a soft breeze strummed on harps of pine trees, while linnets, white-throated sparrows, and grosbeaks sang into the still loveliness.

Then into the scene came the clown, the joker, like the court fool of olden days. A loon flew low over the water like a winged arrow, uttering his half-hysterical cries and laughter. Without reducing his speed in the least, he dived directly into the lake, disappearing completely. Up he came now, skimming across the surface and beating the water with his wings, his cries more weird than ever. Alternately he flew, dived, swam in craziest manner, shrieking, calling, laughing wildly. His voice echoed along the lake shores. He answered the echo and the echo answered him until the region fairly vibrated with his voice.

We laughed. This was a royal welcome indeed, and this bit of clowning by the loon added zest to it.

And now as we put out from shore in our canoe, gliding silently over what seemed to be a lake of gold, we knew well there were more events of surprise and delight to come. Our canoe trail would lead us from this lake, whose shores we had reached by a narrow woods road, through a charming channel into another lake where no road had yet touched. In this second lake nestled a little tree-covered island, and upon it stood a cabin that was tiny too. This was the aim and end of our journey.

Our hearts were beating hard when we rounded the last point of land and the island came to view. It, too, had been prettied up by nature for our homecoming. The sun was a great red ball at the western horizon. It peered through the pine trees as if it were stealing one last look before retiring. Our clowning loon shot through the sky overhead, screaming in wild happiness.

"He's just telling them all we have arrived," affirmed Giny. "Certainly makes us feel important, doesn't it?"

How we hoped that his calls *would* tell many that we had arrived. Those wooded shores about us were the homes of some very precious forest people!

"There is a deer!" exclaimed Giny, pointing to the shadowed depths of a little bay. "Could it be Bobette?"

It *could* be Bobette, though we could not know for sure. This was where Bobette had lived when we knew her and petted her as a fawn. The woods back of the bay were sacred to us, too, for in them had lived Inky the porcupine. Inky, the old rascal porky, who had given us so many lessons, and so many problems, during the time we raised him and turned him loose in the forest. Inky of the sharp teeth, Inky of the many quills, Inky with a sense of humor that had made him an expert and adorable pest. Would he still be there and would he know us?

"And there is that high ridge of maple trees where we always thought Rack and Ruin lived," exclaimed Giny excitedly, pointing to some distant groves. Yes, Rack and Ruin our friendly raccoons had lived some-where in that region. Would they still be there, and would they know us? Would Sausage our woodchuck come back to be our friend again? Only the hours and days to come could give us our answers.

But now we were approaching our island, and our eyes, ears and thoughts strained with anticipation.

"Oh, I wonder!—I wonder if Salt and Pepper are there!" whispered Giny hesitantly, as if she feared she might get the wrong answer. "What a climax it would be to all this wonderful welcome if we see them again!"

"I predict you will see plenty of them before this season is over—maybe too much!" I replied, and my words were much truer than I realized.

Six months before we had left Salt and Pepper, two young porcupines then half a year of age, on our island. From the time they were three weeks old they had been our pets. Our experience with Inky had given us an appetite for porky companionship. Inky alone had taught us many things of the character of his kind. We had found him intelligent and devoted to us. But we had learned nothing of the ways of porcupines with one another. Hence when forest rangers offered us two baby porcupines orphaned by a forest tragedy, we eagerly accepted them. Through that summer we had played with them, worked with them, watched them, until they were as deeply imbedded in our hearts as Inky was. Then when winter work called us, we had to leave them behind to their own very capable devices.

But now it seemed that this might have occurred long ago, so many things had happened. Bobby, the grand lad who had been so much a part of life at the Sanctuary, had answered the call of his country, and, with typical character and courage, was flying with the air force. Giny and I had traveled thousands of miles in public service, and met thousands of people. But the memory of those two porcupines and their friendly devotion was still vivid with us. And that day as we returned home, we wondered about these two creatures more than all the others. Would they be there on the island where we had last seen them? Would they know us? Would we still have the somewhat painful pleasure of bites from their sharp teeth and pricks from their needle-like quills?

We had not long to wait for our answer. The island was now about one hundred yards ahead of us. We scanned the shores carefully, and strained our eyes looking at the tops of trees where our odd little pets had lived. Giny could not resist the urge to call.

"Salt and Pepper!" Her voice carried far in the silence. "Salt and Pepper—are you there?"

We stopped paddling and listened. It seemed that everything else stopped and listened, too. The whole forest was suddenly silent.

Across the waters came the unmistakable call of a porcupine, emanating from the trees on our island. Then a second porcupine voice joined the first, and the two continued in ever-increasing excitement. How well we knew those voices, and the meaning of their tones! Those were the *happy* notes of our porky pets, the way they talked when they saw us on a trail, or took favorite food from our hands, or met us at our doorway in early morning. It was the kind of call they used to awaken us in the middle of the night (when we would rather have been allowed to sleep), the call that made us leave our dinner table to feed or play with those pestersome but precious porcupine pets.

Yes, Salt and Pepper were there on the island waiting for us! They had met the many problems of the winter, proved their independence of our help, and yet had not forgotten us. And the miracle of it was that they had remembered our voices! In no other way could they have identified us that evening of our return. It was not possible that they could have seen us so far away. Nor could they have caught our scent, as there was no breeze to carry it to them. Only the call Giny had made gave them news of our coming. But they knew her voice, and associated with it the many happy events of our months together—events which must have been as enjoyable for them as for us.

Needless to say, we increased our pace. Our paddles set the image of the sky to rocking, and the canoe bow cut through the reflection of the sunset. Constantly the porcupines called to us, their voices conveying excitement in ever-rising pitch. They became still more excited as we called back in their language—and let it be said we can talk pretty good *Porcupinese!*

When we reached the island and guided the canoe into the shore-line sands, Salt and Pepper were at the water's edge to meet us. They could not wait for us to land. With uncontrolled enthusiasm they climbed over the bow of the canoe, over the luggage—and all over us!

What a welcome it was! We were smothered and monopolized with porcupine caresses. Gone, for a time, were all poetic thoughts, wasted all the beauty of that forest festival! All we could see were those excited, animated bundles of quills and hair climbing up our arms, on our shoulders, and all over our heads. All we could feel were those strong porcupine claws gripping and scratching our necks and faces, while chisel-like teeth nibbled at our heads and ears. Grunty talk of the jubilant porcupines was mingled with our own futile objections and requests for moderation. It was all in wondrous good fellowship no doubt—but we would have preferred that our little friends like us not quite so much all at one time.

That habit of chewing on our heads was the one thing we had hoped they had forgotten—but they hadn't. It was their favorite occupation, and our pet peeve. Up on our shoulders they would climb, grunting in most happy manner, and there sit as if they had received the extreme blessing of creation—nibbling at our scalps. And really, that wasn't very complimentary to us, as they are naturally bark eaters. No doubt they were seeking the salt on our skin. But whatever the purpose, they persisted in their head chewing, whether we liked it or not.

How those little rascals had grown! When at last we

19

were able to get out of the canoe and put them on the ground, we were simply amazed at their size. True, they were not full grown yet, as a porcupine does not reach maturity for about three years, but they had changed greatly from the immature little walking pin-cushions we had left on the island six months before.

But we had more to do at that moment than stand and stare at a couple of porcupines. Darkness was creeping through the forest, and we had yet to establish ourselves in our cabin.

"All right, you fellows," I said to them, with an assumed authority which I alone felt. "Out of the way now! We must move in this baggage, build fires, get dinner, and do a lot of things more important than playing around with you."

But they had no notion of getting out of the way. In fact, they embarked upon a campaign designed to interfere with everything we wanted to do. Everywhere I wanted to step, there was a porcupine. Every suitcase or duffle bag I reached for had a porcupine on it. Every time I stooped over, one or both of them climbed up on my back. And I was picking up and putting down porcupines, chasing them away from cameras, typewriters, brief cases and other damageable articles, stumbling over them or dancing around to keep from stepping on them, until I wished every one of their twelve thousand quills was turned around and sticking in them.

It is one of life's richest joys to return to a woodland cabin after an absence. The comfort, security, rest and freedom that is represented in such a little woodland home is carried in our hearts as a memory and a promise. Now we had returned. The promises and plans of months were fulfilled. We were on our cabin doorstep once more.

Again, it was like the atmosphere of a well-planned surprise party. We turned the key in the lock, and stood back while the door swung open slowly. It seemed that a thousand voices of memories cried "Surprise!" There was our fireplace, which had given us so many happy hours and now openly promised as many more. There was the kitchen which, viewed with a north-woods appetite, produced miracles in meals. There were our shelves of books holding out to us measureless information, inspiration and rich thought. And there was that *quiet* which was such a contrast to the nervous, noisy, hurrying world we had left behind.

But Salt and Pepper did not permit our meditation to go far. As we stood on the doorstep for this brief moment enjoying the sensation of our return, they suddenly dashed by our feet and into the house. They were grunting wildly their delight at finding the door open to them. It never had been before! Maybe these human beings had learned something while they were away. For in times past we had been quite careful to keep them out of our cabin. Their home was the woods, and we did not want to create in them a taste for the unnecessary comforts our way of living might offer them. We had had sufficient experience in raising Inky in a cabin. Not an article of furniture had escaped his autograph—carved by his sharp teeth. Hence, Salt and Pepper had been taught to regard the trees, or the space beneath the cabin, as their dwelling places.

But that door had constituted a challenge to them. Time and again it had been shut (perhaps rudely) in their faces. It had been the place where we had disappeared when they wanted to follow us. It was the place where they stood and called, generally with success, when they wanted tasty bites of food. There was something mysterious about it. Maybe it led into another world, or to a porcupine heaven—who could know? Hence, when they found it open, it seemed to be some grand opportunity that might only knock once!

Into the door they went, not even hesitating to take a bite at the suitcases which sat close at hand. And after them we went, knowing from experience what porcupine teeth can do in a very few minutes. But they were not going to be taken easily. Outside they would have stopped immediately, always anxious for us to take them in our arms. Not so in the cabin! We reached for them and they dodged under articles of furniture. We pleaded with them, but they did not respond. We threatened them, and they cared not. Under chairs, over rugs, in and out of corners, behind doors and cupboards the race went, Giny and I the pursuers, they the pursued. Giny and I were much in earnest, but the porcupines were having a wonderful time. We left the door open, hoping they would go out, but they wouldn't go near it. We offered them cookies, but they

wouldn't take a bite. Instead the little rascals ran excitedly over or under everything, biting left and right, until they finished exhausted in one corner breathing heavily, while Giny and I were in another corner in the same condition.

At last, with tact, strategy and a measure of good luck, Giny caught Pepper and carried the grunting and biting animal out of doors. Salt saw the fate of his comrade and retreated under a low bed, where he established himself defensively, nose tucked between his front feet, quills bristling, tail lashing back and forth menacingly.

Now I am sure getting a porcupine out from under a low bed must be one of life's most intricate problems. I would like to counsel with one of our military strategists on the matter sometime to see if he could suggest an effective approach. Salt was thoroughly conscious of his advantageous position. He knew I could come at him from only one direction, and in that direction he pointed his tail and all of his thousands of quills. And he loved the contest. He would not permit himself to be ignored. Sensing the hopelessness of a direct attack, I tried letting him alone for a while, thinking he might come out. Instead, he began chewing on the bed, and slivers from its finely finished wood began dropping on the floor. This brought me into action again, much to his delight. He was playing, I knew, but my task could not have been more difficult if he had been in deadly earnest. I reached for him, and got several quills in my hand for my trouble. I tried to move him with my foot, but he simply climbed on it and began chewing my shoe. I started to push him out with a broom, but he screamed so loudly that I gave that up. Apparently this was against the rules of this little game he had invented, and which I had to play whether I liked it or not.

Giny began preparing dinner, while I continued

with my perplexing problem. If I left Salt for a moment, slivers started coming out of the bed again. Using my best porcupine talk, I coaxed him. He talked right back in his happiest grunts, but not a step did he move. With sudden inspiration I moved the bed—but he moved right along with it. I became desperate. There seemed to be only one way to remove that porky without calling out the militia, and I realized what that was. Without further hesitation I tore the bed apart. Dust covers, mattress, springs, slats, railings, I snatched from over him, until Salt, surprised and a bit resentful, stood in the midst of the floor fully exposed, his protective covering absolutely gone. He did not know what had happened or where to run. Seizing upon his moment of bewilderment, I picked him up and carried him outdoors in spite of his screaming, scratching and biting. I put him on the ground and made a run for the door. So did he. I had never seen a porcupine move so fast before. But I beat him, and slammed the door against his sensitive and obtrusive nose. Pepper joined him and the two of them sat in consultation, telling us plainly what they thought of our lack of hospitality.

Giny and I were tired, very tired, as we sat at dinner.

"Well, anyway," I suggested, "this was a mighty nice welcome the north woods gave us."

"Yes," agreed Giny, with a sigh, "but just a little bit overseasoned—too much Salt and Pepper."

"Yes, I know," I said laughing. "But we know we like them, pestiferous as they are. No doubt they will have plenty of tricks to use on us in the morning."

But Salt and Pepper had no notion of waiting until morning!

II

CRUNCH, CRUNCH AND *DOUBLE CRUNCH*

FOR WEEKS we had been looking forward with joy to the rest that would be ours when we arrived at our Sanctuary. We knew well the quiet and peace which awaited us. In noisy cities where sound sleep was almost impossible, we would comfort ourselves with the thought of our north-woods home. There we would be free from the excitement and pressure of city life. There we would doze away to the lullaby of the wind in the pines. There we would know a dreamless sleep in a seamless silence.

And that first night of our return, we set about to collect this promised sleep. We were right tired by the time the most necessary things had been done that first evening. We went to bed, and were just entering the pearly gates of our dreamland paradise, when there came a sound so penetrating it seemed to bore right into our thoughts.

C-r-u-n-c-h! C-r-u-n-c-h! C-r-u-n-c-h!

Salt was chewing at the front doorsill, methodically, persistently, in a way that seemed to promise that though it might take a long time, he would heroically persist until he had chewed the house down. I beat the floor vigorously with my boot. There was profound silence for a moment, and then——

C-r-u-n-c-h! C-r-u-n-c-h! C-r-u-n-c-h!

Pepper was chewing at the back doorsill at about the same pace and persistence Salt had initiated, as if she would eat her way along until she met him at about the middle of the cabin. Again my boot came into service, and after the floor had received another good beating there was quiet. For a moment we thought we had triumphed, and we had started seeking that elusive sleep again, when came——

D-o-u-b-l-e c-r-u-n-c-h! D-o-u-b-l-e c-r-u-n-c-h! D-o-u-b-l-e c-r-u-n-c-h!

Salt and Pepper were chewing a duet on their respective doorsills! Now the annoyance of a porky's chewing is not measured entirely by the sound. There is a threat to his nibbling that denies one any possible comfort while it is going on. Those sharp amber-colored teeth of his can cut through anything that is not made of metal. It always seems that he is working on the last quarter inch of the foundation of the cabin itself, and any bite may be the final one that produces a complete collapse. If the *crunch, crunch, crunch* were not associated with a porcupine, if it were being sung by a phonograph, likely we could ignore it, or bury our heads beneath a pillow and forget it. But because of the calamity this gnawing promises, we find ourselves propped up on our elbows, listening to it, hoping each of its gripping notes will be the last, and knowing full well that it won't be.

I gave the floor several more good beatings with my boot, and thereby gained some moments of silence. But then again would come that *C-r-u-n-c-h, c-r-u-nc-h,* and *d-o-u-b-l-e c-r-u-n-c-h.* There was nothing to do but get up. Certainly, that is what Salt and Pepper were working for. They didn't care a thing about those doorsills. The sills had been there all winter, and they had not given them a nip. But they knew that inside those doors were their newly returned human friends. They knew they had been without our companionship long enough. And probably they knew that their gnawing sooner or later would get them the attention they wanted.

Grudgingly I went out to play with them for a while. They romped with me, climbed over me and chewed at the back of my head. It was a lovely night —moon and stars shining—and I might have forgiven them at any other time. But now we wanted that promised sleep, that rest to which we had been looking forward.

Then an idea came to me. There had been arranged for these porcupines just one place where they could go under the house. It was not a large opening, and I could easily block it. Giving them one final tussle, I gathered them up, and before they could form any possible objections I had tucked them under the house, and placed a log at the opening. Now! There they could stay until morning, and let doorsills alone—also let us have some sleep.

Again we had tiptoed almost to dreamland, the peace and silence of the forest was ours at last—when——

C-r-u-n-c-h! C-r-u-n-c-h! C-r-u-n-c-h!

Yes, and *d-o-u-b-l-e c-r-u-n-c-h, d-o-u-b-l-e c-r-u-n-c-h,* too!

Right under our beds they had started chewing on the floor joist! It was a hundredfold more intimate and threatening than the nibbling of the doorsills had been, and they interspersed the *crunching* with occasional conversation and calls! There were violent beatings on the floors with boots and other articles—but these gained only momentary relief. Before the new spasm had subsided I was outside again, kneeling at the opening which led under the house, having hurriedly removed the log I had placed there, literally begging Salt and Pepper to come on out and play with me—but to let the house alone.

The moon had traveled far in its course across the heavens and daylight was rather close at hand before the two pesky porcupines developed a hunger for some wild cherry twigs, and climbed into a tree near the cabin. We wearily went to gather the remaining fragments of our coveted sleep.

The next day came all too quickly, and with it much to be done. Salt and Pepper didn't care, though. They slept through most of the sunlight hours anyway, that they might be bright and fresh for their work on the doorsills and floor joist in nights to come.

When the excitement of the first several days had passed at the Sanctuary, we found time to look around a bit. The forest world was sparkling with spring.

Buds were swelling, grasses were greening, spring peepers calling, and bird travelers arriving and looking around energetically for accommodations. Many were making our little island their home. Perhaps they felt the safety of the place; perhaps they were attracted by the feeding station, bird bath and bird hotels we kept ready for their use. Maybe the rich growth of berry trees and bushes was to their liking. Whatever brought them, brought us happiness too.

Eagerly we watched them as they moved in. Some were old friends, some new friends; all were welcome. We saw the purple finch select the crotch of a white birch tree as a homesite, and we knew then that our mornings and evenings would be saturated with one of the sweetest songs of the wild wood. We saw the song sparrow eying with satisfaction a low balsam tree near the water's edge, and we knew that soon his bouncing happy song would adorn the solitude. The trim little white-throated sparrow found a hollow stump to his liking. Everything already lovely in the wildwood would be made lovelier by his plaintive, sweet: "Poor John Pea-bo-dy, Pea-bo-dy, Pea-bo-dy." Phoebe returned again to a favorite spot under the eaves of our boathouse, where she had nested for three years. An oriole chose the delicate drooping limbs of a yellow birch as the building site of her remarkable woven house. A warbling vireo moved into a wild cherry tree. An oven bird selected the grasses on a little hillside in which to build that funny little nest that looks like a Dutch oven. Tree swallows moved into hollows in dead trees in a near-by swamp; red-winged blackbirds nested in tangled swamp shrubbery near them; martins entered the home prepared for them at the tip of another small island, while the inevitable robins were everywhere. Certainly we were not going to want for bird music in the weeks ahead.

We were not going to want for other woodland interest either. The whole Sanctuary was rich with promise. Beavers had established themselves in a little cove we called Beaver Bay. We found evidence of their presence in freshly cut trees along the shores and up the creek, and in floating sticks of aspen from which the bark had been removed by their sharp teeth.

Bears were in the region of Vanishing Lake. Along the trail to the little lake were several trees having their unmistakable marks. Nature students are not in agreement as to the motive bears have in making such marks. The powerful creatures fly at a tree as if they were going to pull it to pieces. They will strike it with their ponderous paws, cut deep gashes in the bark with their claws. Not infrequently they bite into the tree savagely, growling in apparent fury, tearing out great pieces of wood. Some say this is a way of showing off before a mate. Others believe it is posting a challenge to other bears who might invade forbidden territory. Still others believe the purpose, at least in part, is to obtain the medicinal sap of the tree, as bears are seen to come back to trees so treated and lick at the wounds they have made. Perhaps all these purposes are involved. But at least, as far as we were concerned, it was a message that these interesting animals were in our forest.

Near the bear trees there were curious marks on small balsams. These also told us a story. Long scratches ran lengthwise of the little trees, beginning at a point about three feet high, and running almost to the ground—the autograph of a wildcat, left as the beautiful but cunning creature had yawned and stretched and reached for something on which to try his claws, even as our domestic cats do.

At the base of a white spruce which towered over a hundred feet high were several holes cut deeply into the tree. The holes were fully two inches across at the opening, and reached a depth of about three inches into the tree. On the ground beneath them was a pile of chips, some of the slivers large enough to do credit to the gnawing of our porcupines. But this was the work of the great pileated woodpecker, which is exceeded in size only by the ivory-billed woodpecker of the South. He looks to be fully as large as a crow, his head crested with red, and there is no more happy or industrious workman in all the forest. Chanting incessantly, he bores quickly into the trees, making the chips fly and letting them fall where they may, while he feasts upon insects and grubs he is finding.

What grand things we had to watch that season! What pleasure it would be to spy on these creatures, watch their ways, and maybe learn some things we had not known before!

Along the north shore of our lake one of those first

days we found the footprint of an enormous buck! Hurriedly we landed and examined the tracks. We could see where the creature had come down to the water to drink, had wandered along the sandy shore for fifty yards, and then returned into the woods. Likely this visit had happened but a short time before. The footprints of a deer are not at all rare in those sands and usually such markings would have drawn no more than passing notice from us. But these tracks were of deeper interest. They were tremendous in size.

"The Antlered King?" queried Giny as we noted the great spread and depth of the hoofmarks.

Perhaps! We could not know from tracks alone. But certainly such a track could indicate the presence of that greatest of all bucks whom we had named the Antlered King. Two years before we had seen him on several occasions. No adventure at the Sanctuary was more prized than those moments when we looked upon this magnificent creature, who was so much larger than others of his kind that it seemed he might have been of another species. He was a leftover from the earlier years, when many living things of the forest were of greater strength and stature. Then a year passed in which we did not see him at all. We feared something had happened to him. But now these tracks—had he returned?

One evening Giny and I sat before the fireplace,

35

making notes of the many things developing in the woodland world about us.

"There is so much in this great show nature is staging for us that it seems a shame others are not here to enjoy it," I ventured with conviction.

Giny's eyes lit with interest.

"Yes," I continued, "there should be someone with us—perhaps a youth. Someone to ask funny questions and make us think hard to give the answers. Someone to tip things over accidentally, to get in funny kinds of trouble——"

"You are missing Bobby, aren't you?" Giny interrupted.

I nodded.

"Why, there hasn't been a thing dropped or broken or spilled since we arrived. No one has tipped over the coffee pot, no one has fallen in the lake, no one has put salt in the sugar bowl—I tell you, it is monotonous!"

But Giny was not listening to me. She had risen, walked over to the desk, and begun writing a letter. I watched her, awaiting an explanation which was not to come. With an air of affected aloofness she sealed the envelope and stamped it.

"Am I to know anything about that letter?" I finally asked.

"Maybe!" With studied indifference she placed the envelope in her handbag, obviously to keep me from seeing the address.

"When?"

"Oh—sometime."

"Is something going to happen because of that letter?"

"I hope so."

"Will I like what happens?"

"I hope so," she said.

III

SUCH LANGUAGE!

EACH day was bulging with events and adventure, so that the mysterious letter was half forgotten. Interest in the matter was suddenly revived, however, when Giny snatched from one morning's mail an envelope bringing a reply to what she had written. Again she wrote and mailed a letter of which I was refused the slightest information. In helplessness, I left the matter to developments.

A survey of the trees of the island made me somewhat uncomfortably conscious of the nibblings and gnawings our porky friends had done during the winter. They had bitten their autographs into almost everything they could reach. Numerous trees had been scarred—balsams, birches, cedars, white and red pines, cherries, maples, oaks. There seemed to be none immune. Most of the trees were not seriously injured. Many had been bitten slightly at one small spot, as if the porcupines were only tasting them. However, one red pine that stood beside our little back porch had been completely peeled of bark from top to bottom! It was a lusty young pine, some forty feet high, and we disliked losing it. We told the porkies so. In fact, we gave them a mighty severe reprimand, to which they listened with interest—then decided we were playing with them, and started a lively romp.

But we knew well that if we were not prepared to stand such losses we had no right to have porcupines for pets. Their friendship must be rated as worth this cost or not accepted at all. After all, no matter how friendly they might be with us, they were still porcupines and must live as porkies. Bark is their principal winter food. When snows are deep and travel difficult, a porcupine will select a tree to his particular liking, climb in it and live there perhaps for several weeks. During this time he will scale the bark from the tree, eating much of it. Of course, the tree cannot live after that. Our fine red pine was gone. But Salt and Pepper had behaved simply as porcupines. It was nothing to them that the tree was one of our favorites. They were born to an infinite forest, and all trees were created for their use—as near as they could tell. Furthermore, in nature's over-all plan porcupines benefit the woods by their gnawings. They thin out timber stands so that there will be fewer trees perhaps, but far better ones. Before we criticize them too harshly let us remind ourselves that the grandest forests in the world have reached their perfection while porcupines lived within them—and men did not.

Gradually Salt and Pepper were weaned away from

their gnawing at the door and the floor joist. When they found we were not going away again they were not so anxious to be with us every moment. Besides, they need not spend all their time and energy in chewing tasteless old boards; they had found a new diversion. Screen doors had been hung, and screens placed on the windows. The doors especially made wonderful scratching, and this different kind of a sound got them very quick results.

As the nights grew warmer and windows were left open, they formed another habit which ultimately caused us considerable embarrassment with our neighbors. In the evening, especially when Giny and I would be talking or reading aloud, they would climb into a tree just outside our window and enter into the conversation in a most disconcerting way. Right in the midst of our words they would break in with that little *Honk! Honk! Honk!* of theirs, and continue it so insistently that sometimes we had to give up.

One night Giny was reading from Emerson's essay "Self-Reliance." She had reached those very wise words where this great man tells us something we should all know: "There is a time in every man's education when he arrives at the conviction that envy is ignorance, that imitation is suicide. . . ."

Honk! Honk! Honk! Honk! This sound came from a tree outside the window. Giny added power to her tones, determined not to be interrupted.

"That he must accept himself for better or for worse as his portion, and though . . ."

Honk! Honk! Honk! Honk!

"And though the wide universe is full of good, no kernel of nourishing corn can come to him except through his toil . . ."

Honk! Honk! Honk! Honk! Honk!

Giny drew a deep breath and stubbornly continued, ". . . . except through his toil bestowed upon that plot of ground which is given him to till. . . . None but he . . ."

Honk! Honk! Honk! Honk! Honk!

". . . none but he can know what that is that he can do . . ."

Honk, honk

". . . nor does he . . ."

Honk! Honk! Honk!

". . . nor does he know until he has tried!" During the last words Giny's voice had increased until she was fairly shouting.

Honk! Honk! Honk! Honk! came the rising cries from outside the window.

"Salt and Pepper, such manners!" Giny started a reprimand that was never finished. The porcupines, hearing words addressed to them, turned loose an avalanche of *honks* that monopolized the occasion.

More and more we were seeing the great difference

in the two porcupines. Salt, although the male, was the more affectionate of the two, wanting always to be with us. He liked to be cuddled. When we would take him in our arms and, regardless of sharp quills, squeeze him to us, he would relax, let out a sigh of contentment, and remain perfectly still as long as we held him.

One night Giny took him in her arms and, swinging him back and forth as one would a baby, sang a little lullaby. That was just grand for Salt! Back he came the next night at about the same time for an encore. Giny obliged him. After that he came every evening expecting this bit of mothering. He would refuse food, or any other kind of attention, until Giny put him through his lullaby.

Pepper, the female, leaned more toward the wilderness. She sought the tops of tall trees, explored the mystery of brush and logs. Salt would leave whatever he was doing—even his sleeping, which was his principal occupation—to pester us and play with us. Not so with Pepper. We were a mere incident in her life, and not the sole object of her affections. She would come to us, behaving at such times somewhat as Salt did, but always with much more reserve. Frequently we found her in trees at the far points of the island, and by her manner she showed us clearly she would rather not be disturbed. Sometimes she would be in the shallow waters at the shore line, looking in the direction of the great forest on the mainland, silently listening and seemingly yearning for the adventures she might find there.

But Salt was much more contented with his island, and with us. It was he who was watching for the door to open so that he could pounce upon us. It was he who would chew on our window sill in the middle of the night, and call to us whenever he heard us. Yes, and many times when he didn't!

During these days we were learning more of the language of the porcupine. He has a surprising variety of tones, calls, expressions, each with a specific meaning. One still night we heard a startling scream coming from a stand of pine trees on the mainland. We could not identify it. The quality of the voice suggested a porcupine, but neither Giny nor I had ever heard one make a noise like that. It seemed to be a distress cry, not unlike the shriek of an excited monkey. Several times the cry was repeated. So certain did I feel that some creature was in serious agony that I went forth in my canoe to investigate. When I landed on the far shore, the cry ceased for a time. Then suddenly it issued forth from a tree almost directly over my head. With my flashlight I searched about the foliage. The startling cry was given once more, and there in the crotch of a tree I discovered an enormous old porcupine, perfectly relaxed and certainly the picture of comfort. His eyes were closed, and he seemed to be asleep.

As I watched him, he gave the maudlin cry again. He did not even lift his head or open his eyes. Perhaps he was undergoing a porcupine nightmare; maybe he dreamed he was a wildcat, and if so, he was doing a right good job at impersonating one. I wanted to make sure he was all right, so I tossed sticks up in the foliage near him. He stirred himself, got to his feet, looked down at me resentfully, and then with fine agility climbed higher to another crotch, where he settled in comfort. Clearly there was nothing wrong with him.

As I went back to my canoe, he gave that weird cry again. I do not know its meaning. Maybe it is the most far-reaching call for a mate. Maybe it is simply the animal's effort to express himself. Perhaps it is a challenge to his enemies. Whatever the purpose of it may be, it is one of the most moving calls I have known in the forest, even challenging the fearful shriek of the lynx for wild fury.

We have never heard Salt or Pepper give this cry. However, there was something of it in Salt's voice whenever Pepper had wandered away from him. At such times his calls had a touch of loneliness in them. His voice would begin high, descending the scale in little staccato grunts, the quality of which could arise only from a lonely heart.

We knew well their little play talk that went on as they scuffled with each other. It was a mumbling, grumbling series of sounds that were playfully resentful. We knew the cross tone that seemed to say, "Let me alone and get away from here"—this one uttered by the first one who tired of playing and wanted to quit. We knew their hunger call, which told us to bring them some bread, some cookies or some peanuts. We knew and loved their soft notes of contentment, their highest expression of happiness, uttered when they were given liberty to chew our hair and bite the backs of our heads. And we knew well the little grunts of happiness that were uttered when anything pleased them.

Through knowing the meaning of their calls, we could understand something of what went on in their minds. One day we had enticed Pepper into a sunny spot to take pictures of her. The sun was hot that spring day, and if there is one thing that a porcupine likes less than all others it is hot sun. We lured Pepper into desired poses by offering bites of tasty food, and by petting and playing with her. But all the time she was blinking discontentedly, and becoming very tired of the sun. Of a sudden she became animated with decision. She faced about, pointing toward a shed underneath which the ground would be cool and where the sun could not shine. Then she gave a series of those little happiness grunts. Unquestionably she had thought of this place where she could be more comfortable. It takes a lot to make a porcupine run, but she ran that day—straight to that shed and far back under it. We could not coax her out for the rest of the day.

And because we know what this little talk means, we were able to interpret another adventure one of those first evenings. Hoping always for our many forest friends to come to us, we had been placing a pan of food out near our island cabin every night. In the previous season creatures from the mainland had been regular customers at this outdoor cafeteria. One of our favorite sights was to see a circle of raccoons about the pan, with Salt and Pepper trying hard to edge their way in and get some food that they wouldn't have eaten at all if they had not believed others wanted it.

We had just retired that night when we heard Salt and Pepper scuffling, giving their competitive little calls as they tried to bite and push each other around. Suddenly this call ceased, and we heard the little happy grunt. Something had happened to please them greatly. The change in their mood was so sudden it puzzled us. We arose and tiptoed to the open window, all the while hearing their happy call. There we saw what

had so delighted them. The raccoons had returned, probably for the first time since the previous autumn. Salt and Pepper had remembered their friends and obviously were glad to see them. The raccoons, too, were giving a dainty trill, which is their manner of expressing pleasure. It was plain that these creatures had formed a happy acquaintance and possibly a real friendship.

But in truth, we human beings know only enough about the language of animals to understand that there is much to learn. We know the purring of a cat means contentment, and we know how the same creature cries when in distress. We understand some of the expressions of dogs—their little barks of happiness when things are right, their whines and howls of discontent when things are not so good. A hunter knows well the baying of his hound when the creature is following a trail, and he understands the short sharp barks when the dog has treed his game. A farmer knows the meaning of the mooing of his cow, and the whinny of his horse. A woodsman hears the howling of a wolf, the bark of a fox, and can be fairly sure what these creatures are saying. Yet, at best we are only catching a word here and there of a vast animal language. There are things we can observe but cannot explain. We do not understand how creatures communicate complete ideas. We cannot explain how a doe instructs her fawn in absolute silence. We do not know what call assembles conventions of animals—rabbits, squirrels, birds—and sometimes leads them to great migrations. On occasions when we see great flocks of wild geese flying as do our planes in V-shaped battle formation, we hear their calls, their commands. But what has brought them together, by what method they have chosen their leader, how all know where they are going—this is beyond our knowledge. And by what method do the birds pass around word that our feeding station has been opened for business? The first day food is put out, perhaps three or four drop in. But within a week there will be scores of them. Some way the news has been spread around. And there is that remarkable observation about ants, when one of them, having discovered a huge bit of food too large for him to lift, returns to his colony and gets help. What does he do to present the problem to his fellows? How does he say the equivalent of "Come on, Jim, Jack, Hortense and Percival—I need your help." Yet, in some manner he does it, for a right number of helpers will follow him to the burden and bring it in.

Yes, there is much more going on in this world of nature than most people suppose. We have caught a few audible words of a vast and universal language. There is no such thing as dumb animals, unless it may be that we are pretty dumb when we call them that.

IV

MAGIC NIGHT WITH MONKEYSHINES

Aw! Balsam Juice!

THERE are times in forest life that are made just for unusual adventure. One who lives in the woods quickly recognizes such charmed hours. I doubt if anyone can say just what distinguishes them. Nevertheless, occasionally there is a sacred something in the mood of nature which promises great things. All the little living things fall under this spell, and the whole woodland world moves in mysterious ways about one common purpose. While we often feel this mood during daylight hours, it reaches its height only as darkness creeps over the forest world. *Magic Night* is the name we have for such precious periods, and it does seem then that the fairies, gnomes, nymphs and spirits created by human imagination might come trooping out of secret doors in trees and rocks, or come sliding down on star beams.

That spring a Magic Night came to the Sanctuary. Giny recognized it and called me to look out our door into the gathering gloom. Salt and Pepper for once were quiet! They stretched out on the limb of a tree, feet hanging down, eyes open, just looking and listening into the night.

"There will be adventure in the forest tonight," Giny affirmed.

The sky had blushed beautifully at the last caress of the sun, and now an afterglow held at the horizon as if nature were clinging to her memory of day. Venus, the evening star, was shining like a jewel worn on the breast of night. The sweet breath of the forest bore the pungent perfume of countless woodland blossoms. A pleasant nocturnal chill crept over the earth, and a mist began to rise like a veil nature was drawing across her face.

"The night is calling—shall we go?" I asked.

But Giny did not wish to go. She had writing to do, she said. I knew well about that writing. Another of those mysterious letters had arrived, and must be answered. My questions always drew the same evasive answers, the same provoking wink and smile, so I had learned it was futile to press the matter.

"Then, if you do not mind, I shall go alone," I said. "We must not waste a Magic Night, you know."

"Please do!" insisted Giny. "And I'll be waiting to hear of your adventure."

I walked through the darkness to the shore where my canoe was always waiting. Salt and Pepper never stirred as I passed beneath them.

"Would that *I* could charm them as this night has

done!" I thought, recalling their nibblings and gnaw-ings. But I knew this power would never be mine.

For a moment I stood beside the canoe drinking in the growing glory about me. In the distance a great horned owl haunted the rich gloom with his hollow voice. Tree toads were calling; there came the last sleepy notes of a robin. Some creature—a deer or a bear—was wading along in shallow waters on a distant shore, splashing musically. Back of all else was the rhythmic murmur of hordes of insects. In the dark these sounds seemed unattached, as if the night itself thus spoke in countless tongues.

Now I slipped the canoe into the water, and sculling silently over the smooth surface, approached the main-land. Towering trees loomed like a great cloud over me as I neared shore. Back of me now lay the island, silhouetted against the afterglow, the lighted cabin windows looking like little peepholes in the darkness through which we might see into a realm of even greater glory. And I remember saying quietly to my-self, "I wonder if there is anything in creation more beautiful than that: a cabin with lighted windows, standing on a pine-covered island, silhouetted against the afterglow—seen on a Magic Night!"

Some way it seemed to be the meeting point of what is human in nature and what is natural in man, reveal-ing that which is Divine.

I landed and walked through the darkness along the

trail that circles our mainland cabin. No need to use the flashlight I carried in my pocket. I knew every foot of this trail, every bush, every tree. I knew when I was at the hillside where Bobette the fawn had loved to sun herself, knew when I passed the little animal runway where Rack and Ruin the raccoons came and went, knew when I was approaching the old red pine stump on which had been placed a cake of salt as an offering to all visiting creatures—but particularly as a gift to Inky the porcupine.

But here something caused me to stop and listen. There was a creature at the salt lick! First I heard the rustling about in leaves that might have been caused by almost any kind of animal. I listened anxiously. Then came sounds which left no doubt of the iden-tity of the sound maker. *C-r-u-n-c-h! C-r-u-n-c-h! C-r-u-n-c-h!* as chisel-like teeth bit into the wood of the salt-soaked stump, and then I heard the soft, happy grunts of a porcupine! Could this possibly be my old friend Inky? My heart pounded with delight.

Suppressing excitement as best I could, I gave the porcupine call—the one for companionship or atten-tion. The crunching stopped; so did the happy grunts.

"Inky!" I ventured his name, and then followed with a message in porcupinese.

There was no reply immediately. However, neither was there a hurried flight by the animal, and this en-couraged me. Taking one cautious step at a time, I moved toward the salt lick. It was now about thirty feet away. All the while I was talking my most cultured porcupinese, interspersed with a few enticing human words.

Within about ten feet of the stump I paused. Still there was no sound from the creature. I turned on my flashlight. There sat an enormous old porky looking calmly and inquisitively in my direction. I was convinced!

"Inky! Inky—you blessed old scamp, is it you?"

He did not move. This assured me more than anything else that it was he. A wilder creature would be gone before this. I approached him cautiously, talking constantly in soft tones. Finally, after I had emitted a long series of porky words intended to be happy grunts, he made several little sounds in reply!

Fully confident now that this was my pet, I knelt near him. Not more than three feet separated us. He did not move. I reached out a hand and he sniffed at it. I touched his nose, and then cautiously smoothed down the coarse quills that crowned his head. For just a moment this extreme intimacy frightened him. Long life in the forest had nearly erased from his memory this manner of greeting. He started up as if to run away. But he stopped and turned toward me again. *Honk! Honk! Honk! Honk.* His calls became more strong and confident. He was remembering me. Four years now this little creature had lived a normal porcupine life in the forest. Four years of problems which daily directed him to develop and depend upon his instincts. Yet the love he had established in his heart for human friends lived on!

And there we sat that Magic Night—a porcupine and a man—our world for the moment a tiny bubble of light the flashlight made in an infinitude of darkness, but each one happy in his own way that he had found the other.

"Inky, you bedraggled, quill-covered, ornery-looking old rascal!" said I, accustomed to abusing those I love. "I never saw anything in my life that looked worse and yet looked better to me than you."

In times past I always had given Inky the power of human speech in my imagination. We had carried on many a fancied conversation together. That Magic Night he gained voice once more, in the same way.

"Well, Sammy, old kid!" he replied with a twitch of his nose. "You wouldn't take any prizes in a porcupine beauty contest yourself, you white-skinned, thin-haired, dull-toothed, earth-bound scamp. It's right good to see you. Bend over here while I set a quill in your ear, just for old time's sake!"

"You would, you bum!" I said, taking care that he did not get hold of me. "Stand still while I look you over. What a whopper you are!"

Inky was an enormous porcupine. I looked at him in amazement. He would weigh well over twenty pounds, and his great coat of quills made him look much heavier than that. His quills were very coarse, some of them four inches long, and light in color so that he presented a gray appearance. His babyhood blackness that had earned him the name of Inky had entirely vanished.

Now he became a bit bolder, apparently recalling more and more of our friendship. I had dropped to sitting position on the ground. He moved to me, step at a time, until his front feet were in my lap, and he was looking into my face, freely talking his happy grunts. I grunted right back at him. How I wished I could really learn from him his adventures during those long months in the forest! What fine sights he must have seen from his perch high in a tree!

"Seems to me," he said, "seems to me you talk better porky than you used to. Lost some of that human accent."

"I'm having lots of practice these days, Inky." I was stroking his head again. "Have you heard about Salt and Pepper?"

"Humph! I've heard about 'em." He shook his quills in obvious disgust. "A couple of young punks, if you ask me. Is that the best you could get?"

I laughed. "Inky, I do believe you are jealous!"

"What! Jealous of those young twig-chewers?" He chattered his teeth. "Bet I can girdle a maple tree faster than they can bite off a lily pad!"

A look at the great amber-colored teeth at the front of Inky's mouth would suggest that this might be true.

"But they skinned a forty-foot red pine for me," I taunted.

"Aw! Balsam Juice! It took two of 'em to do it, didn't it? Someday come back and see the white pine I skinned all by myself! One of your big ones—out near Vanishing Lake. I tell you it would take a dozen of those little monkeys to make one good porcupine!" And of a sudden he flew into a spasm of his old-time toughness, whirling, whirling, first one way, then the other, lashing back and forth with his tail and chattering his teeth. I laughed at his antics. How well I remembered how he used to execute this dervish dance on our cabin floor, sending us up on chairs or anywhere to get out of his way! I told him I would have to admit that he was quite a porcupine.

But right when Inky's dance was at its height, there came the sound of breaking twigs back in the forest. Inky heard it, and stopped to listen. There were more sounds—some heavy creature was coming. Inky made a dash for a tree and climbed to safety.

"So long, old top," I whispered. "I'll meet you here again."

"That's a date," said Inky, and so it proved to be on many occasions that summer.

Now I moved back of a bit of brush, shut off the flashlight, and waited. Closer and closer came the sound trail of the newcomer, moving unhurriedly, but steadily. I heard the leaves stir on the ground, heard twigs crack, heard bushes rustle as something forced a way through them. At last the sounds were right at the salt lick. I turned on the flashlight.

There stood a magnificent doe! The light did not frighten her in the least. She was pawing at the stump a little, and licking the wood below the cake of salt. Occasionally she lifted her beautiful head and looked alertly into the night. Her great cupped ears turned constantly, pointing ahead, to the sides, and even back of her, as she kept the whole forest under attention.

57

An idea came to me, though perhaps I was expecting too much of this Magic Night. Could this be Bobette? If Inky had held his liking for our Sanctuary, and had made the salt lick a calling place, would it be impossible that our fawn should do the same?

"Bobette!" My voice trembled a little. "Bobette!"

The doe's ears came forward and she was all attention. Yet, despite my anxiety, I could not accept this as proof. Any deer would have reacted in the same way to any sound.

"Bobette, is that you?"

I asked the question with all my heart, and yet I knew that I would never have an answer. There was no mark nor manner about this lovely creature that would prove it was our former friend. We had no language in common. The deer is the most silent of all forest creatures, having no sound other than the whistling snort which is given in alarm. I could not grunt out a conversation as with Inky. The most satisfaction I could know was that it *could* be Bobette there before me. This was a big doe. Bobette would be of good size now, for she would be four years old. This creature had come from the direction of the valley in which Bobette had made her wildwood home. She had come to the cabin where Bobette had been cared for as a fawn. It could be—and I felt happiness even in the possibility.

The doe finished her refreshment at the salt lick.

Unhurriedly she moved into the dark forest from which she had come. I could follow her far into the dark distance by the sounds of breaking twigs, rustling leaves and brush. Perhaps there was a tiny spotted baby of hers back in there somewhere, curled up on the ground implicitly obeying orders to remain absolutely silent until the mother's return.

Giny listened to a detailed account of the adventure as we sat before a dancing grate fire. She was delighted to hear of Inky's presence.

"And couldn't we just call this doe Bobette?" she asked. "You know it could be."

"Bobette is a good name for any deer," I commented, and from that night on, any deer seen at that salt lick was Bobette so far as we were concerned.

"And now," said I, with a meaning look, "you have written another letter. Am I to learn anything about that mystery?"

There came that smile and sly wink. "Not even a Magic Night can get you that," said Giny.

"That's what I thought!" said I, resignedly.

V

A TENT HOUSE FOR CAROL

ONE sunny morning, a few days after the Magic
Night with Inky, I was wasting my time in a most
capable way, trying to get Salt and Pepper to pose for
a motion picture. Particularly did I want to record
the highly amusing way they would sometimes box
with each other. We had watched it often. I presume
there was a measure of ill-humor involved in it, for
their talk at the time was not made of those happy

grunts. It resembled the resentful blast of a cat whose
dignity had been offended. The two porcupines would
sit facing each other, striking out harmlessly with their

front feet, apparently not liking the experience in particular, but each one too stubborn to withdraw.

That morning I had noticed them start their comic boxing match. I ran out with my camera, but immediately they stopped. When I came in to put the camera away they started again. Once more I ran out ready to take pictures, but the opportunity was gone. I tried to provoke the mimic battle by placing them before each other, but they were not in the mood. No sooner would I get Salt in position than Pepper would run away. When I had retrieved Pepper, Salt would dash for the underbrush.

Suddenly I noticed Giny was standing in the cabin doorway laughing at my futile efforts.

"Do I hear any helpful suggestions?" I asked.

"None—but I have a bit of news for you." She came out of the door, carrying a newly opened letter in her hand.

"The mystery of those letters is about to be cleared up," I guessed, as Pepper ended all hope of picture-taking by racing up a tall birch tree, while Salt, suddenly becoming affectionate, was climbing to my shoulder, grunting soft nothings in my ear.

Giny nodded. "Do you remember the day you wished for someone to join us here, the day you were so lonely for Bobby, and said we should have someone around to laugh and to get in trouble?"

I did.

"Well, you are to get your wish. Carol is coming!"

"Carol? You mean our little Carol? Coming here?" I could hardly believe it.

"Yes, I mean our little Carol. She is coming in late August. All those letters were extending an invitation, getting her parents' consent, arranging the date and such things. Are you pleased?"

I was more than pleased, I was jubilant.

"Salt, do you hear?" I cried as I picked the surprised porcupine off my shoulder and raised him to arms' length overhead. "Carol is coming!"

If it is possible for a porcupine to say "So what?" with a look, Salt did it. Who was this Carol person, whose very coming stirred up things so he must be snatched away from chewing my head, and waved about in the air?

Well, Salt, if you knew Carol you would be as stirred by the news of her coming as were Giny and I. Carol was then a lovely girl of high-school age who had already proved her ability to be sweet without weakness, beautiful without self-consciousness, intelligent without conceit. We had first noticed her when she was still a grade-school child. She had attended a lecture in which we had shown pictures of the Sanctuary animals. She was so taken with Inky, Rack and Ruin, Bobette and Sausage that she squealed with delight when she saw them. Her enthusiasm and animation put us all to laughing. Undoubtedly that evening brought her parents many new problems. She must have a porcupine pet. She must have some raccoons. She wanted some bears. Already, they informed us, their home had been an asylum for every kind of creature Carol had found —dogs, cats, birds, turtles, mice, bugs and most everything but snakes. That night she became so insistent upon having these new pets that the situation almost got out of control. To quiet her, Giny and I said that *maybe* someday she could come up to the Sanctuary and see our friends. This little proposition, given in the best of faith, did not calm matters in the least. It merely made her break out with her enthusiasm in another direction. All right! She would come. When would it be? Next week? Next month? Should she start getting her things ready?

Carol was finally quieted for that night, but she had taken our invitation seriously, and indeed we had meant it that way. Nothing could give us greater happiness than to have a visitor who loved nature the way she did. But our place is not suited to tiny tots. Carol must grow a bit first.

I fear when this was told to Carol, she spent much of her time trying to grow to Sanctuary requirements. Often we heard from her. Whenever I gave a lecture within reach of her home, she attended. We knew of her graduating from grade school, and of her first days in high. But the many new things which came into her life did not dim her enthusiasm for nature, nor did she forget that "someday she was coming to the Sanctuary." If there was any change, it was only that she became more excited about the idea. At the close of her freshman year she asked if she might come. but we felt that she was still too young to exercise the judgment necessary in our work with those animals. After her sophomore year she might have been qualified, but we were away. Now she was in her junior year, and still the flame of interest and enthusiasm burned on. Nor had our desire to have her been reduced in the least. In fact, I think we were as anxious and excited about it as she was. But a new obstacle had presented itself. Out of patriotic duty, Carol had devoted her vacation time to war work. It seemed the right thing to do, and undoubtedly it was.

"You will understand it if I read you parts of her letter," Giny was saying. "Just listen to this. She says, 'Yes, I can come. It won't be for long, just a week—but what a week it will be! Mother says I need this rest before school starts. But oh, I wonder if that week will ever come. It seems so far away. In school I used to try to understand those long periods of geological time, eons, ages and such things. Now I know how long they are—like the time between now and when I come up to the Sanctuary. I'll be there, like a whirlwind!'"

I laughed, placing the objecting Salt on the ground. That described it—Carol would come like a whirlwind. But it would be a blessed, beautiful whirlwind, stirring up that forest world to happier living.

"The mystery of your letter writing comes to a happy ending," I said to Giny. "It was a grand idea! But now I have an idea, too—Carol shall have a tent house!"

"A penthouse?" Giny misunderstood.

"No—a *tent* house," I laughed. "I know of a manufacturer who makes a tent in the form of a house. Carol shall have a cabin of her own, close enough to ours so she will not be afraid."

Another exchange of letters brought Carol's approval of this idea. A cabin of her own, a canvas cabin among pine trees—nothing could please her more.

It was some weeks before Carol would arrive, but there was much to be done. First we ordered the tent house, and in the course of a few days it arrived, knocked down, crated in a long box.

It was rather a hopeless array of varied-length sticks and rolls of canvas we looked upon when we opened the box. But if we did our work well when we had finished bolting together the woodwork, laying down the floor, and stretching the prepared strips of canvas in proper place, Carol would have awaiting her a clean, comfortable cabin twelve feet long and eight feet wide. It would be weather-tight, and mosquito-tight. It would be almost touching our cabin.

Putting that tent house together was quite a job.

Giny and I were the construction engineers and the labor crew. We said later we could have done the whole thing in one-third the time if we hadn't had some help. The more help we received, the more difficult the job. For our help came, unsolicited and unwanted, from Salt and Pepper!

The sight of all that new, clean wood, and rolls of brown canvas was too much for them. They actually became bewildered as to what to bite first. We almost gave up. It took nearly all of our time keeping those porkies away from our new equipment. They chewed the canvas roofing, they bit the wooden beams, they gnawed the bottom of a nail sack so that the nails poured out on the ground. It was a field day for them. What more could they want? All these grand things to chew, and their human friends staying with them hour after hour—just to play! And play it was—for them! When we would push them away, they would whirl around and act *tough*. When we would jump to save some priceless bit of equipment from their devastating teeth, they loved the attention and would go nosing about *honking* happily.

Boards had to be sawed at proper length to make the floor. No sooner had I started to do this, than here came two porcupines on the run. Two children headed for a Halloween party could not have looked happier than they, and for the same impish reason. Salt paused long enough on his way to tip over a small can of paint that had carelessly been left on the ground. I jumped to grab it and save as much of it as possible— and that wasn't very much. While I went to put the nearly empty can in a shed, Salt proceeded to wade in the paint that had been spilled. When I next saw him he was leaving a trail of green after him, and headed straight for a roll of our nice new canvas. I grabbed an old rag, ran frantically to him and threw it over him. Then I picked him up and carried him away. He was *honking* his happiest and biting his best. Scolding him constantly and futilely, I wiped the paint from his feet and tail as best I could.

A call came from Giny. "You had better see what Pepper is doing over at the flooring—she is awfully quiet!"

She was quiet, all right, but not idle. The handle of my saw had been chewed halfway through, and when I arrived she was just finishing the complete demolishment of the pencil I had been using for marking the boards. I carried her away (not too gently, I fear) and hung her far out on the limb of a tree. I hurried back to get a stroke or two of sawing done before she could return—and there sat Salt on the flooring, chewing away at the bits of pencil he could find, and still having enough green paint on him to leave a footprint everywhere he stepped! Before I could pick him up, Pepper had come back and, with fiendish delight, climbed up on the boards. I wouldn't have minded so much, except they insisted on being right where I wanted to saw.

I am sure it was one of the happiest moments of their lives, and let me add that the pleasure was all theirs. If Rome wasn't built in a day, as the saying goes, I'll wager it was because there were some porcupines around. Once I carried them down the trail to the far part of the island, left them there and hurried to my sawing. They almost beat me back! The only way I ever got that sawing done was to put the two pests on my shoulders and let them chew on my head to their hearts' content. And if you think that is a comfortable way to work, just try it sometime. Finally the flooring was sawed, but it looked as if it had been done with a can opener!

It wasn't only with the sawing that Salt and Pepper "helped." When Giny and I were bolting the framework together, it was a golden opportunity for their talents. What a mess of things to bite, and what countless places to be! Every time we tried to drive a nail, a porcupine suddenly appeared on top of it. If we wanted to tighten a bolt, one of them would try to do it with his teeth. Whenever a new beam or rafter was put in position, both Salt and Pepper would have to climb on it to see that it was in proper place. If we stooped over, they would climb on our backs; if we knelt down, they thought we were playing with them and they would go whirling around acting *tough* all over the place. Once, when I had been on my knees nailing flooring for some time and had become a bit tired, I decided to rest for a few moments, and sat down —right on a porcupine! I didn't stay there long. And through it all we listened to more porcupine grunts than we had heard in all our previous experience. They were the happy grunts. This was life as they thought it should be lived.

It speaks well for our endurance that we finally finished erecting Carol's tent house. It was endurance that did it. We did not outwit our porcupine helpers, nor did we master them—we simply outlasted them. By midafternoon they were exhausted, which fact shows there is some justice in the world. They dragged themselves slowly and regretfully away, climbed into a tree and went to sleep. Giny and I would have liked to climb into a tree also, if that meant rest. But this was our opportunity, and we called forth our last bit of reserve strength to take advantage of it. The framework of the tent house had been completed, and the canvas stretched on just as darkness closed over the world. And if the sun had been as tired as we were it would have skipped next day—that is, unless it had two porcupines calling to it the way Salt and Pepper called to us a very, very few hours later.

That tent house stands today, with porky teeth marks in its framework, porky teeth holes in its canvas, porky footprints in green paint on its floor, but in all we feel that it is a monument to our own perseverance—and we are proud of it.

VI

THE WAY OF WILD HEARTS

A Porky Pines

FOR Carol the next few weeks in the city dragged along as if they were trailing an anchor. She tried to shorten that "geological period" between the accepted invitation and the day of her coming by writing letters. What should she bring? What should she wear? Did we suppose it was going to rain? At what time would her train arrive, and why couldn't it get there sooner? Who would meet her at the station? Could Salt come? What were we going to do the first day, the second day, the other days? Could she learn to chop wood with a saw, or saw it with an ax—she wasn't sure which was right. She wanted to swim, hike, climb trees, be on the go early and late—in fact, she designed a program of events that would have worn out a regiment of soldiers. She wanted to know all about her tent house, and her letter fairly squealed with excitement after our detailed description. We had no doubt of the wild and happy time we were in for when that little tornado struck the Sanctuary. Giny expressed it well when someone asked her who our much-talked-of guest was to be.

"There will be about half a dozen people called Carol," she said, and so it proved to be.

While Giny and I were anxious for Carol's coming, time did not drag at the Sanctuary. Salt and Pepper saw to that. Their resources for giving us problems were simply inexhaustible. Sometimes it was because of what they did, sometimes what they didn't do. Sometimes it was that they were too much in evidence, sometimes because they couldn't be found at all.

Right now they were preparing for us a new adventure, having in it pleasure with a bit of pain, a sweetness that was just a little sad.

The poor old porcupine has never been thought of as having much affection for his kind, or in fact for anything else. His supposed indifference and stupidity have been the joke and jibe of nature students. But in Inky, our solitary porcupine pet, we had found an ability to form a friendship which endured. In Salt and Pepper was a repetition of the friendship, but also living evidence of their devotion to each other.

Sometimes the wild heart rings truer than our own. Numerous and gripping are the stories of devotion between creatures, often in odd combinations.

On a midwestern farm a few years ago a collie dog struck up a friendship with a huge stray cat. The cat appeared about the barn, apparently intent upon staying. The dog was delighted, but not the farmer. Times were hard at this farm, where there were many to feed, and even one extra cat would burden them. The cat remained for several weeks, mostly because of the insistence of the dog. But one day Old Tommy, as he had been named, was taken away to another farm several miles distant, where an overpopulation of rats and mice offered him considerable employment. Yet the cat found no contentment at his new home, and spent most of his time *miaowing* his loneliness. The collie dog back at the other farm became despondent. He refused to eat, spending all his time searching for Old Tommy. One day the dog disappeared. He was gone for several days, then reappeared trotting happily up the roadway—Old Tommy beside him! It was an experience which touched the heart of the farmer. Nevertheless, Old Tommy was taken back to the second farm once more. Again the collie retrieved him. Then in desperation, the farmer took Old Tommy to a third farm, about six miles away. It was a larger problem for the collie this time, but he was equal to it. He was gone for over a week before he returned—with Old Tommy trotting by his side. The farmer gave in then, and Old Tommy was allowed to stay, much to the delight of the collie and himself.

At the home of a friend of mine I saw a black cat (named Rastus) and a gorgeous yellow canary (named Lucky) form an attachment for each other that was amazing. Lucky always enjoyed the freedom of the house. A few appealing peeps from him would bring someone to open the door of his cage so that he might fly anywhere he pleased. Sometimes his choice was a perch on the chandelier, sometimes on the head or shoulder of a human friend, sometimes he preferred to take a bath in a water glass on the dinner table, or sit on the side of a plate and pick up bits from a vegetable salad. But sooner or later he would go in search of Rastus. Finding the cat, he would emit a number of happy little notes, and light between the two black ears of the cat. Immediately the cat would begin purring! It was a strange sight to see two creatures, often enemies, so devoted. At sleepy time in the evening, neither the cat nor the bird would go to bed without the other. Rastus had appropriated for himself a big luxurious chair in the parlor. At the right hour he would climb into this chair, but instead of curling up and going to sleep in that wonderful, relaxed cat fashion, he would begin a teasing *miaow*. This would continue until Lucky was brought, cage and all, and placed near him. Then the air would be filled with *purrs* by Rastus and *peeps* by Lucky, until the two fell into a sleep that was enriched by their fine friendship.

On a stock farm in a prairie state, a small monkey appeared one day. Nothing was ever learned of his history. Perhaps he had escaped from a circus. Perhaps he had been a pet of some traveler. Whatever was his story, he appeared at this farm, riding on the back of a cow! It was something of a shock for the farmer, living far from the country where monkeys grow, to see one suddenly so much at home with his domestic animals. The farm animals seemed to think nothing of it, however. The monkey, named Mike by his new friends, was perfectly at home with cows, horses, pigs, chickens, ducks and the farm dog. They liked him and he liked them. In fact, his affection for his animal associates was a source of considerable trouble for the farmer. Mike didn't want these pals of his disturbed. He didn't want the cows to be milked. He didn't want the pigs put in their pen. When the farmer would come to get the pigs from the hickory grove where they were often allowed to roam, the monkey would chase them to the far corners of the field. As the farmer approached, Mike would jump at the porkers, scream-

ing and striking at them, sending them away on the run. And it was not uncommon to see him grab the tail of a running pig, swing himself upon the porker's back, and go riding away in Wild-West style. Mike stayed on into the winter, sleeping at night on the back of a cow where he would be warm. The farmer took a liking to him and tried to be patient with his many pranks, but some of the things the little monkey did would exasperate a saint. So much did Mike object to the farmer milking the cows, that frequently he would grab the man's hat and run with it to the top of a tall oak tree. There he would deposit it, wedging it firmly in a crotch. The farmer spent much of his time climbing high after his hat and other small articles of clothing. When many such annoyances forced him to do so, the man had the monkey taken to a zoo. There Mike is with others of his kind, and no doubt he is telling them many stories about the fine fellows he found at that farm—and how the cruel farmer would pinch a cow until milk came!

One of the most amusing bits of mothering I have seen was a cat who adopted a family of young ducks. It was strange indeed to see her go along talking in the same tones she would have used with kittens, the ducks waddling along at either side, behind, and beneath her. Her worries were intensified when her adopted youngsters quite naturally took to swimming in a little pool, while she stood at the edge held back by her inborn dis-

like for water, calling to her charges instructions and
cautions that fell on deaf ears.

So many are these stories that no animal lover will
doubt for a moment the ability of these so-called dumb
creatures to manifest the highest order of devotion. Of
course, most such stories are about those animals nearest us—the domestic or tame ones. But the little wild
folk are no different. We cannot see so clearly into
their lives, but we see enough to know that the same
fine character is there, and that sometimes companionship is so important to them that they do not care to live
if it is broken.

A hunter, walking along the shore of a frozen northern lake, was attracted by the hectic and unsteady flight
of a duck. The bird circled about, calling constantly,
and did not dart through the sky in the arrowlike style
typical of his kind. Besides, it was late for such birds
to be in that country; they should have gone south long
before. Soon the man discovered what was bothering
the duck. On the ice was another duck, probably the
mate, and obviously in trouble. The bird would try to
fly, but could not rise. The hunter was not a very good
sportsman, as events disclosed. Intent only upon getting the duck, he made his way across the ice. As he
did, the bird overhead circled low over him, apparently trying to draw his attention. But he went on,
reached the helpless bird, and killed it with a stick. As
he returned to shore, the other duck came in and landed

near him. It made no effort to escape as he ran toward it, but quietly waited for the blow of the stick which ended its life. The man later expressed his regret that he had killed the birds, for he said that most certainly those ducks had refused to be separated even at the cost of their lives.

On a backwoods road in a Western national park, two rangers were driving along in a car on fire-patrol duty. The road, not being graveled or paved, had two very deep ruts in it, cut by automobile wheels. Suddenly ahead of them, the men saw a big mother rabbit come out of the brush, followed by half a dozen little woolly youngsters. The mother skipped over the road easily, leading the way, but the little ones did not do so well. The rut was too deep and too wide for their tiny jumps. Into it they tumbled, and their troubles began. Time and again they tried to climb the walls of dirt, only to fall back. They raced up and down their troublesome trench looking for lower places, but they found none. The rangers had stopped their car to take in the amusing show. But when it seemed sure that the little fellows were not going to get out under their own power, the men left their car and started walking toward the animals, intent upon helping them. The mother rabbit did not understand their move. Suddenly she appeared in the middle of the road directly in front of the men, all prepared to fight. She bared her teeth, raced nervously back and forth, and showed plainly that if those men wanted to hurt her babies they would have to deal with her first. The men stopped in admiration at this display of courage and devotion. In the meantime, the little fellows obviously were inspired by the actions of their gallant mother. By supreme effort, they scratched, kicked and scrambled out of the rut and ran into the woods. Then the brave mother followed them. As the rangers went back to the car, one of them said, "I am glad I saw that in person, for if you had told me about it, I wouldn't have believed you." The other one said he was having a hard time to believe his own eyes.

Salt and Pepper lived in fine companionship from the very first. They played together constantly, and, during the early months at least, were inseparable. Of course, they had their little quarrels, which were never serious.

Springtime had now ripened into summer. June rains had finished, and the long lazy days and warm nights of July had come to the Sanctuary. The protected waters in shallow bays were becoming speckled with lily pads, while slender blades of basket grass floated on the surface pointing the direction of the current.

Now we were seeing the individuality of our porky pets come forth. Salt, although the male, was the stay-at-home, the one contented with his island life. He held to the trees close to our cabin, and it was he who was forever calling to us in the middle of the night, or pestering us through the day. Pepper, however, had reached a point where she seldom called to us, her attention directed out into the mysterious distance and vastness of the forest. She haunted the far corners of the island, climbed to dizzy heights in the trees, and at times waded in the shallow waters along the island shores as if striving to get up enough courage to swim away. Between the two porcupines there had developed a mental tug-of-war. Salt was forever coaxing her to the cabin, calling to her, and trying to keep her within the sphere of his interest. Sometimes he succeeded in influencing her briefly, and bringing her to our doorstep where they would scuffle as in their baby days. But presently Pepper would turn away, sniff the breeze, and start for the deep brush or tall trees. Sometimes she could coax Salt away with her, take him exploring, perhaps to show him how much larger the world was than he had supposed. But he was not content to stay away from us for long. Day after day we watched this contention grow between them. Unquestionably they wanted the society of each other. Their little grunts of happiness when they were together showed that. But something was reaching out of the wilderness and drawing Pepper, while Salt's heart was devoted to the Sanctuary.

"I believe she is hearing the call of the wild," said Giny one star-lit evening, as we watched Pepper astride the low limb of a tree, looking and listening into the silence. Certainly everything about the creature suggested fascinated attention. Her eyes were open wide as if they could see through the darkness, her nostrils working to analyze scents beyond our ken. We called to her, but she did not respond, nor even look our way. Salt played at our feet, grunted a greeting and climbed to my shoulder to chew methodically at my head. Whatever the spell that held Pepper, it did not touch Salt.

Nature students are sometimes led to wonder if animals do not have abilities unexplained by the action of the five senses as we know them. There is a rich and beautiful veil of mystery between the grand drama of nature and ourselves. We human beings may as well be honest and admit that we know very little of the why and wherefore of what we see. We are spectators of marvelous happenings, but our explanations are only guesses. What impulse compels the migrations of birds and butterflies? What directs the miraculous flight of a bee? Whence come the laws which govern the civilization of ants? What guides the salmon to the river of his birth? A thousand other unanswered questions remind us that our knowledge of such things is little, even though our interest is great. And sometimes we try to dismiss those doings of the wild folk by calling it "instinct"—which is a cover-all word for that which we do not understand.

We realized our questions about Pepper would never

be answered. Something, we knew not what, was reaching out of the forest or out of her own nature and drawing her away from us. We felt the distance grow between us. Her effort to take Salt along was obvious and continuous. So was his effort to hold her back.

"Someday she is going to leave," said Giny, a tone of sadness in her voice. "Whatever that call may be, it is too strong."

It happened sooner than we anticipated. Summer was still young when there came another Magic Night. The veil of mystery hung over the north country, and the silence that is more than silence reigned everywhere. It was the kind of night when strange things happen. Pepper was restless and excited. She came to the house and ate sparingly of a cookie we gave her. For a brief moment she played with Salt. Then she went up a tree—he went to sleep.

The still night was ideal for canoeing, and Giny and I sculled our light craft about the north shore of our lake. Half a dozen deer appeared like ghosts in the edge of the water. We saw a beaver, a muskrat, heard a bear, and felt everywhere the charm that enchanted the forest. When we returned to the island there was a strange and empty feeling about the place. We both felt it. Salt met us at the dock, acting oddly. He talked incessantly, a new note in his voice. The usual things did not please him. I raised him to my shoulder, but he did not wish to remain there, and was not interested in chewing on my head. He followed us to the cabin, but refused the bite of cookie we offered him.

Giny stood looking at him intently for a moment. "Do you know," she said, "I believe Pepper is gone!" We searched the island, looking up trees that had been favorite spots of Pepper, peering under boathouse and cabin, calling constantly. Salt trailed along with us, adding his call to ours. But the night gave us no answer. There was only the drip of dew, only the rustle of deer mice in dry leaves, only the echoes of our own voices.

Salt was most distressed. His little talk became almost a wail. Not a thing we could do gave him the least bit of comfort. Pepper was gone. In vain she had tried to pull him with her. But the call which was reaching her heart was one that must be obeyed. She was going into the wilderness, with Salt if he would go, without him if he would not. At the moment he was not ready to give up his attachment to the cabin and his human friends. So, she had gone without him, but she had left a most miserable porcupine pal behind her.

It was because of Salt's unhappiness that we continued our search. We felt no concern about Pepper. In fact, we had hoped both porkies would lead normal lives, that they would take to the forest, remembering us only sufficiently to permit us to keep account of them. We thought that the parting would be easy, that we could see them swim away and have perfect contentment in the thought of them living naturally. But we had not figured that one would be left behind, so torn with loneliness that it troubled our hearts.

We showered Salt with condolences, but it did no good. Our petting and caresses were not what he wanted. I presume a porcupine cannot cry tears. But there were tears in Salt's voice if not in his eyes. We could hardly stand his grief. Out we went in our canoe, determined to bring Pepper back if possible. We cruised the shores of the lake, not knowing what direction she might have gone, calling constantly. But never a reply did we get, except from an old blue heron whom we disturbed. He flew up and over our heads, telling us a few things which fortunately we did not understand. We landed on the mainland and walked the trails, calling for Pepper in both English and Porcupinese. As we neared the salt lick, a porky voice answered us. Excitedly, we turned a flashlight in the direction of the call. There stood old Inky, looking at us with his shoe-button eyes.

"Hi, kids!" he seemed to say. "What's bein' baked, boiled, fried or broiled?"

"Inky, boy—Pepper is gone," I said, moving toward him. "Have you seen anything of her?"

"You know everything, Inky. Where is Pepper?" Giny added, dropping to the ground near him.

Inky moved slowly toward me, a step at a time, until

I touched him with my hand. Then suddenly he became *tough,* and started whirling around.

"Inky!" I said, a bit hurt. "This is no time for play. We need your help. Pepper is gone. We can't find her anywhere."

He looked up at me as if to say, "So what? That's no loss."

"Yes, but, Inky, it's serious. Salt is over there on the island with his heart broken."

"Aw! Balsam Juice!" Inky was tougher than ever. "Don't get so riled up about those sentimental young upstarts. They can figure it out for themselves. They aren't handicapped like you human beings. The only way you get any news is by talkin' or writin', hearin', or seein' something. Those young punks don't amount to much, but they are smarter than you are. Let 'em alone. What if Salt is lonesome? It's good for him. He'll hear from Pepper someday, and in a way that you couldn't understand. He'll be pulling out himself pretty soon, and I wouldn't be surprised if both of them chisel in on my salt lick."

We were quiet while Inky continued waltzing around. Suddenly he looked up.

"Looks as if he were sorry for us now," said Giny.

Yes, it did. Inky looked serious, almost apologetic. He rose on his hind legs, shook out his great coat of quills, and looked the words:

"Aw, I suppose I'm too rough with you folks. I

don't mean to be. But you human beings seem to be so stupid. You've been leanin' on different kinds of crutches so long you have lost some of your natural ability. You don't know how to feel things. You can't look out into the night and just know what is going on. You don't listen to the little voices inside yourselves that will tell you everything you ought to know. I understand you human beings haven't always been so stupid. You used to be smarter than you are now. You had what you call instincts, as we do. Maybe you had intuition, too; I don't know. But you don't have to be responsible for us. We can take care of ourselves. Pepper will know where to go and when to come back. Something inside her will tell her. And as for that whimperin' young imp over on the island, I'd like to give him some extra quills with my compliments."

And Inky flew into another spasm of *toughness*.

"But Inky," said Giny, "Salt is miserable; we just have to take Pepper back to him."

"Aw! Balsam Juice," said Inky, and he waltzed off into the night.

VII

FWEET, *FWEET* FOR FERRY SERVICE

INKY'S abrupt behavior did not banish our sympathy for Salt, however. This little fellow's mental suffering was too obvious, too real.

It was a disconsolate porcupine that met us that night when we returned from our fruitless search for his mate. We could hear his mournful cries long before we reached the island. He was at the landing waiting for us, as if hopeful that we would bring news of Pepper. He followed close at our heels as we walked up the path, talking his sorrow in a way that made us kneel beside him frequently to pet and comfort him. But not even Giny's lullaby song could give him peace. Even as she held him in her arms, swinging him to and fro in the manner that had made him so happy in times past, he emitted his mournful little cries of loneliness.

It may be that we human beings learn things only when facts come to us in a way that hurts a little. It hurt us to see Salt so grieved. We had seen Salt and Pepper play together, and laughed at the fun they were having, but we had not been impressed with the serious and sound nature of their friendship. Now Salt's heartache echoed a pain within our own hearts.

We knew how attached he must have been to be hurt so deeply, and we understood. Never again would we doubt the affection of porcupines for one another. Nor did the fact that Pepper would leave Salt dispute the presence of devotion in her heart. We recalled now how through days and nights she had been endeavoring to take him with her, coaxing him toward the woods. The wilderness had won. Yet we could not doubt that wherever she was, she was enduring the same loneliness we were watching in Salt.

Throughout the remainder of the night Salt called and searched. We heard him under the house, we heard him in the far corners of the island, we heard him high in the trees. For a brief moment there was his *crunch, crunch, crunch* on the front doorsill, but as there was no *double crunch,* he moved on. He gave the screen door only a disinterested passing scratch, took only a halfhearted bite at the floor joist, then wailed on as he explored the dark corners under the cabin.

Dawn found him tired by his ceaseless searching. He climbed to a favorite spot on the cabin roof and sought to lose his sorrow in sleep. But even then he would arouse occasionally and give a pitiful call, beginning high and descending in tone until it ended in a little groan of hopelessness.

Pepper did not return and the experience marked the beginning of maturity for Salt. His baby days were done. He was an adult porcupine now, and must live as such. There were larger problems before him than just to pester us, though he found most effective ways to carry on that, too. Passing days silenced his mourning and in many ways he showed happiness again, but he was never the play-boy porcupine he had been. His affection for us was not changed in the least. He would nestle in our arms, climb to our shoulders, sleep in our laps, and he came regularly for Giny's lullaby ceremony which he loved. But he was very quiet about it all.

"Salt will not be with us long, I think," Giny said. "He is doing the same things Pepper did before she left."

It was now over two weeks since the disappearance of Pepper. We found Salt exploring the extremes of the island, and sometimes in the shallow waters looking and sniffing toward the mainland. Often he lay on that low limb of an oak where Pepper stayed so much, staring out into the darkness and silence of the night. Certainly that mysterious something in nature or within himself which dictates the moves of animals was hard at work.

We were not surprised one night when we returned from a canoe ride to note Salt was not at the dock to meet us. He did not answer our calls. He was not under the cabin, nor on the roof. Bread left on the back step for him had not been touched.

"He's gone!" said Giny with conviction.

Yes, he had gone. We searched the island, but he was not to be found. That which we had hoped for, and yet half dreaded, had happened. He was pushing back his horizons, expanding his world, and this was as we would have it.

"Good-by, Salt," we called into the night, toward the mainland. "Good-by, and remember that means *God be with you.*"

We searched but little for Salt and Pepper after that, though every porcupine we met in the woods during those days was addressed by their names. Many reports were brought to us by people who knew of our pets. A timber cruiser had seen a porcupine near an old deserted cabin, and was startled at the animal's friendliness. We went to the cabin, but the animal had disappeared. A neighbor had a big old porcupine settle under his house, and was astonished when the creature came up and scratched on his door. That scratching sounded promising, and we went on the double quick to this cabin. But the old porcupine we found there resembled neither Salt nor Pepper, and would have nothing to do with us. A fisherman saw two porcupines along a lake shore, and noted how the animals walked far out on a log as if trying to reach his boat. We bent our canoe paddles like bows to reach the place in a hurry, but no porcupines were around.

The news of Salt and Pepper's wanderings produced another sharp reaction. "They can't do that to me!"

wrote Carol, in reply to our letter. "Don't they know it is only 482 hours and 36 minutes until I'll be there? Now it's only 35 minutes. My watch is five minutes slow, so it's only 30. They must hurry back; I want them right where I can grab them up and hug them, quills and all."

We hoped it could be as she wished. But we learn to command nature to do just as she pleases if we want to be obeyed. She does not bend herself to our whims. One realization gave us much satisfaction: if Salt and Pepper, either one or both, were there to greet Carol, it would be from choice. It would not be because they were on an island from which they did not know how to escape. They were on their own now, living a life of freedom and responsibility. They were entirely independent; their decisions and actions would be purely porcupine in nature.

We promised Carol we would wire her if and when the porkies returned.

I have often said that those porcupines had the most uncanny sense of what they shouldn't do, and the greatest determination to do it of any animals I have ever seen. Their sense of humor was mixed with intuition, and a certain maliciousness. They always did what we hoped they wouldn't do. And our next porcupine adventure was certainly of this nature.

Across a little stretch of water from our island, on a

point of land, live our nearest neighbors. They have a lovely little log cabin standing in the midst of stately young red pines. Better neighbors could not be found. They seldom borrow but are always willing to lend. They never impose but are always anxious to favor. They mind their own business and like it. We seldom exchange visits, though through the years we have felt a friendship that is fine and satisfying. The last thing in the world we would want to do is to annoy them or impose on them in any way.

Imagine our concern one fine August evening then, when we were paddling by our neighbor's cabin, and heard him saying in an excited and distressed sort of way, "Now go on, get away. Don't climb on me, I don't want you. Get up a tree. Ouch, stop biting. Get back there and let me alone, or I'll pull every quill out of your hide."

Quills? Biting? Climb a tree? Only one living thing could call for such words!

"We'd better hurry!" said Giny with concern.

I answered with a stroke of my paddle that sent our canoe toward our neighbors' pier. We landed hurriedly and went toward the cabin, flashlights in hand, to find just what we expected and feared. There was Salt, champion pest of the universe, working overtime at his talent! My neighbor had a bucket in his hand, and was trying desperately to get to a near-by pump while Salt whirled about acting *tough* and occasionally making runs at the man. Inside the screen door the lady of the house stood looking out helplessly.

"Is this thing yours?" demanded the man, in tones that were remarkably friendly, everything considered. "If it is, take it away from here. Take it a long way off, and don't let it come back ever."

Yes, that thing was ours! Salt recognized us, and came running to meet us. He grunted happily in greeting and reached up his front feet to be taken.

"Salt, you old scamp!" I said, embarrassed at the whole situation. "Of all places, why did you have to come here? What have you been doing?"

"What has he been doing?" challenged my neighbor. "Just making life miserable for us, that's what." And then while Salt sat contentedly on my shoulder chewing on my head, we listened to a story that made our apologies sound woefully inadequate.

Our neighbors had been sleeping on their screened front porch, resting wonderfully in the famed quiet and coolness of the north woods. Right in the middle of their deepest sleep and finest dreams they had been awakened by a call just outside the screen door. *Honk! Honk! Honk!* had come the sound, sharp and startling in the still night. The people sat up and listened. Again the call, almost beside them. Flashlights were pointed through the screen, and there sat a porcupine looking in at them, obviously quite friendly and not the least bit surprised at what he was doing. Puzzled, our neighbors returned to bed and tried to sleep, saying, "He'll go away in a few minutes." But the porky didn't go away. His calls grew louder and louder. When the neighbors buried their heads under covers to escape from the annoyance, a new sound demanded their attention. *C-r-u-n-c-h! C-r-u-n-c-h! C-r-u-n-c-h!* came from the doorsill. Flashlights were brought into play again, and the man looked upon great slivers of wood being bitten out of his house.

"The blamed idiot was trying to chew his way in!" My neighbor almost shouted as he told the story. He beat on the floor to frighten the porky—but Salt wasn't afraid of that; he had heard me do that so often, he knew there was no danger.

Next Salt demonstrated his ability as a screen scratcher. He clawed and clawed until my neighbor thought the screen would be ripped to ribbons. In one way or another our pesky porky managed to keep our good neighbors awake all night long. The only relief they could get was by throwing some water on Salt, after which he would disappear under the house for a while. But they would hardly have time to close their eyes until *crunch, crunch, crunch, scratch, scratch* and a few *honks* would awaken them again.

When daytime came and my neighbors were moving about their yard, tired from a sleepless night, Salt wanted to play. He ran at them, tried to climb on them, acted *tough* about their feet, and placed himself right in their way wherever they wanted to go.

"Were there—by any chance—two of them?" I asked rather timidly, grieved at their discomfort, but still anxious to know if Pepper were around.

"Thank heavens, no!" thundered my neighbor. "One is enough—one is too much. Take him away from here, and if I never see him again, it will be soon enough."

We carried the contented Salt down to our canoe and paddled toward our island, calling back our apologies as long as we could make ourselves heard.

"Salt, you big bum," I said to the precious pest, as he climbed over my feet talking his happiness constantly, "don't you understand? That is the *one* place you shouldn't go. Those people are friends, they are perfect neighbors, but they didn't invite you there. We don't care what you do to us, for we are interested in studying your ways. But they are here to be quiet and to rest. Why in all this forest did you have to go there?"

But Salt kept right on *honking* his happiness, and took a bite at the railing of the canoe and another at my boot, just to show he wasn't listening to a thing I said.

I looked at him hopelessly, and found myself murmuring in Inky style, "Aw! Balsam Juice!" And that night a telegram went to Carol with the simple message SALT HAS RETURNED.

Our porky was happy to see his island again. He

grunted as we approached the boathouse. He grunted more enthusiastically as he climbed ashore. He went up the trail to the cabin grunting, and grunted more over the bites of food we gave him. There was no question but that he was glad to get back home.

"Then, you old pest, why don't you stay here if you like it so much?"

His answer came the next morning. He was gone again! We called him at breakfast time, but there was no answer. We searched an empty island once more.

"If only he doesn't go back there," said Giny, indicating our neighbor's cabin. I just groaned.

Two days passed in which nothing was heard of our porky. We had found time to read, to photograph some birds, to see the wild asters blooming at the water's edge. Then in the cool of a still evening came a call across the water.

"Ho, there!" It was the voice of our neighbor. Giny and I looked at each other apprehensively.

"Ho, there, Campbells!" the call came again, and we could not dodge the fact that it was for us.

"Yo—we hear you!" I called back, dreading what I knew was coming.

"Well—come—and—get—that—low—down—pest—of—yours." The words came in staccato, with a definite feeling of exasperation in them.

"OK," I called back, trying to be cheerful. "Sorry—I'll—be—right—over!"

I got in a rowboat and went across the stretch of water as fast as I could, one oar squeaking to the rhythm of my strokes. It seemed an endless distance over there, and in my imagination I fancied Salt had my neighbor down jumping on him. No doubt the front door was chewed entirely off the house, the screen stripped to single wires, and many new inventions of impishness carried out by our talented pest.

It was almost that bad. There was Salt acting *tough,* my neighbors looking at him helplessly with no sign of amusement on their faces. They had endured another sleepless night. *Crunching,* chewing, scratching, *honking* had been their lullaby all night long, and it hadn't produced any rest. During the day Salt had rested, but now he was afoot again with such vivaciousness that they feared it prophesied another night without sleep.

"Could you take him and keep him long enough for us to get a little peace?" my neighbor pleaded, his mildness making me feel worse than if he had given me the reprimand I expected. "We are tired, we came here to rest, and we need it."

Bubbling apologies and promises, I took the triumphant Salt on my shoulder, and while he chewed contentedly at my head I got into the boat. He was quite playful and bit at my fingers as I pulled on the oars, chewed at my boots for a moment, acted *tough* a bit, and then went up in the bow where he stood looking toward the approaching island, grunting contentedly. He was happy when he saw the boathouse, happy when he saw Giny, happy when he reached his favorite trees, happy at the cabin door.

"Then why, Salt, why don't you stay here, if you like it so well?" I reasoned with wasted breath. "The one place you shouldn't go, you go. Don't you know that that man would be justified in blasting you out of your hide? The only reason he lets you live is because of his friendship for me."

But it was hopeless. Salt was contented with all that was happening. Even the buckets of water that were being poured on him at the neighbors' cabin were part of the program. At least, he enjoyed the attention.

That night we put him in a cage. We disliked to do it, for we had never kept him confined. But we had to have time to think, to reason our way through the new problem. So we put him in a good-sized pen, gave him plenty of food and water, and left him.

The next morning the wood framework of the cage had been chewed to splinters, the wire cut, and he was gone! We were desperate. That day we went on a porky hunt again. We walked the trails in the forest back of our neighbors; we cruised the shores, calling for Salt, trying to capture him before he went pestering again. Our efforts were utterly useless. Not a sign of him did we see. Hoping against hope, we said perhaps he had gone in another direction this time. But we knew he hadn't—and he hadn't!

"Yoo hoo, Campbells, yoo hoo!" The call came clear and compelling. It was **early** morning, and we were at the breakfast table.

"He's over there," said Giny resignedly.

"Yes," I said, "and it's early morning. Those people do not get up early. Probably Salt has had them awake all night."

"Yoo hoo, Campbells!" came the call again, a little stronger.

I went over, and the worst was true. Salt had put in a marvelous night—my neighbors had put in a miserable one. Buckets of water had failed to drive him away. In fact, he seemed to enjoy the shower bath.

I was humble in my helplessness. Apologies were of no effect. Something had to be done—this could not go on. But I was struck with admiration at my neighbors' good humor.

"I'll get rid of him," I had said, trying to face the problem fairly. "I have no right to annoy you people with my interests and enthusiasms. I'll take him so far he will never get back again."

"No," said my neighbor kindly, "we don't want you to do that. We like Salt—that is, a little. If you will just come and get him quickly, we'll all try to cooperate. Now I found a whistle . . ."

And he exhibited a little metal whistle that had a very shrill note. His idea was that when Salt first appeared he would blow that whistle, and I would come as soon as possible. I thanked him for his kindness and patience, and I agreed to his plan—provided he would promise not to spare me. He must blow that whistle when Salt first appeared, day or night, rain or shine, so that I could remove him in the quickest manner.

"I feel sure he will get over this soon. As fall comes on he will take to the woods, and none of us will see him," I said, speaking my hopes rather than my convictions.

It was agreed that this program would be initiated. To test the whistle for carrying power, he was to try it when I had returned to the island with Salt. Certainly it had a most penetrating tone. I could hear its *f-w-e-e-t, f-w-e-e-t, f-w-e-e-t* as he tried it out, and

99

realized that no sleep, wind or weather could keep the sound from me. I called back an "OK" to my neighbor.

Within two days Salt had left the island. There was delicious silence in his regard for a few hours, and then—

F-w-e-e-t! F-w-e-e-t!

Out I went, as promised, crossing the water in my rowboat with the squeaky oarlock, hurrying to relieve my neighbor of the bequilled pest.

"There he comes to meet you," my neighbor called as I pulled alongside the pier. Sure enough, there came Salt out onto the pier, and into the boat. "He just arrived," commented my neighbor good-naturedly, "and I guess he expected you."

Back I went with Salt to the island. I was grateful that I could get him before much annoyance had been caused. This was going to be a fine system, this whistle plan.

It was a fine thing—if I could endure. For Salt got it into his head that this ferry service was installed for his special benefit. It was his way of getting back to the island. He concluded that it was all right for him to swim away and go off on his secret missions into the forest, but when he wanted to return, the thing to do was to go to my neighbors, *crunch* on his doorsill, scratch his screen, *honk* a few times. Then this man would blow a whistle. Soon he would hear the squeak of an oar, and it was time for him to go down to the pier. Now this boat would come with me in it, and he could get in and have a fine ride back home again. It was all very wonderful—for him. But I was in the same position my neighbor had been. I was begging for sleep. That whistle blew incessantly, it seemed to me. I heard its *f-w-e-e-t, f-w-e-e-t* in the middle of the night, at high noon, in the early morning, in the midst of rains, and I heard it in my dreams when I had a chance to dream.

Once I tried a desperate move. I took Salt away around to the opposite shore of the lake and turned him loose. From here, in order to reach my neighbors, he would have to swim through at least a half mile of water, or walk around a great swamp a distance of three miles or more. From my knowledge of porcupines I felt sure he would not do either. He would establish himself in these new woods, and there he would settle down. I wouldn't see him any more, but even that seemed desirable under present conditions.

Ten days of peace reigned in the Sanctuary. Days were quiet, nights serene.

"I guess we have solved the problem at last," Giny said at breakfast one morning. "Seems a little lonely without Salt, but it is better this way."

I nodded. But even as we sat there, out in the morning air we heard—

F-w-e-e-t! F-w-e-e-t!

"No," said Giny, "it couldn't be that whistle, it must have been a bird."

But *F-w-e-e-t! F-w-e-e-t!* The whistle insisted it was itself in person. Out I went to the rowboat with the squeaky oarlock, and across the water to our neighbors. There was Salt on the pier, grunting his gratitude for the fine ferry service.

"It's a nice day," I called to my neighbor.

"Fine," said he.

"Honk! Honk!" said Salt.

But in the midst of our annoyance, we had to pause and realize what that porcupine had done. At least a three-mile walk through difficult brush-filled woods was necessary to bring him back to this cabin. He had performed something little less than a miracle for a porcupine in thus finding his way. His homing instinct had guided him over ground where woodsmen would have had trouble in traveling. His coming back was a remarkable thing—even though we would rather he had not done it!

VIII

SH–H–H–H!

Carol Learns to Listen

THE day finally came when Carol arrived. We shall never forget it, and it is possible, too, that it is a lasting memory for every animal and plant at the Sanctuary.

Often we have tried to find some similitude with which to compare the energy, pace and excitement of her coming. Perhaps it was like the sudden winds of autumn that stir everything to life, that set the leaves to dancing, trees to bowing, stir the lake to happy racing wavelets, and toss fleecy clouds around in wild merriment. Perhaps it was like the quick and gripping power of that moment when a football team first races upon the field and starts warming up for the contest. Maybe it could be compared with the avalanche which goes tumbling down the mountainside gathering everything into its own vibrant mood. Maybe it was like that carnival spirit which reigns at the big circus when it is suddenly time for hordes of clowns to come running and tumbling about, carrying everyone into their carefree humor.

Yet none of these things quite describes Carol's coming. True, her infectious happiness, her excited interest in everything, suggested the most stirring moments in nature. Carol embodied the very scintillating joy of life, was of the model that talks ahead of her thoughts and says things in a mixed-up way. She was capable of pranks and her capacity for getting into amusing difficulties was inexhaustible—but Carol was a thinker. Always one knew that entwined in that dynamic spirit of hers was an ability to appreciate the finest values in life. Carol was made up in the way more of us should be. She could swim freely in the wholesome fun of life without losing her love of that which is quiet, calm and sweet; she could be serious in her thoughts without losing her joy.

Leaving the Sanctuary before sunrise, I went to meet Carol's train at the village, eleven miles away. The train was scheduled to arrive early—but not early enough for Carol. The conductor remarked that morning that it was the first time they had arrived on time in a month. "We had to!" he explained. "That young lady wouldn't have lived through it if we had been late." There was excitement in the very toot of the train's whistle that morning. The engine came racing into the station, stopped short with squeaking brakes, and stood there puffing as if it had finished a big job with its last bit of strength.

Through the window of the Pullman I could see Carol, waiting with anything but patience while baggage was being unloaded. Her eyes were dancing, and so was she—her lovely loose hair flying this way and that trying to keep up with her gyrations. In vain she was shouting messages to me, the double windows of the car holding back all sound. Other passengers were laughing at her.

The rest of that early morning's experience remains a blur, a blending of suitcases, trunks, Carol's infectious excitement, the smiling porter and conductor, the smiles and waving hands of Carol's newly made friends on the train—and the endless string of questions the child shot at me as we covered the distance to the Sanctuary. Only once was she quiet. As we rounded a curve in the little forest road, there before us stood a beautiful doe! I brought the car to a stop, and the lovely creature stood like a statue, looking at us with curiosity while we looked at her with adoration. Carol could not speak. Her eyes grew wide with wonder, and she uttered a little gasp. After a few moments the doe moved off into the forest. It was only then that Carol could find the power to say, "I have never before seen anything so beautiful."

Her electric mood quickly returned. Each new thing she saw brought forth a fresh outburst of sparkling enthusiasm. The lake, the canoe, the pine-covered shore lines, and at last our island—all seemed to touch off mental bombshells within her.

Giny was there to meet and greet Carol when we landed. So were the chipmunks and red squirrels of

the island, but much to Carol's disappointment Salt
had gone again! There was no time to explain his absence in detail at the moment, but we assured Carol
that it was quite a regular thing and that he would
return.

There was still much of the morning left when we
had breakfasted, and Giny had introduced Carol to her
tent house. She was so happy with her little canvas-
covered home that tears came to her eyes. Giny had
furnished it in bright colors with much thought given
to the things a young girl would like. Carol moved
in, took possession, placed her things about in the way
that pleased her—and said she had never felt more at
home anywhere in her life.

Now we told Carol of our plans designed to give her
the most happiness out of her stay. Each day we were
to take up one new subject in the forest. There would
be time for swimming, hiking, picture taking, play
with the animals—but we would want to be learning
something with our fun.

"It's all fun!" insisted Carol. "But are you sure Salt
will come back?"

Yes, we were sure, unfortunately. Would she see
Pepper? It was possible, though we had not seen her
since her disappearance many weeks before. Would
she see Rack and Ruin? Probably. How about Inky?

"That, Carol, will depend on how well you learn the
lesson we have selected for today," I said.

Carol was all for beginning the lessons at once. She wanted to learn all about everything in nature. What was the subject to be for this first day? Was it to be trees? Flowers? Rocks? Stars? Animals? Was she to learn to tie knots or build fires without matches?

Giny and I laughed.

No, Carol, our subject was of a different nature. It is good to know those things in woods lore, but there are other things in the world of nature more important.

"Today, Carol," I said as she waited for an answer to her many questions, "today we are going to learn to *listen*."

"Learn to listen?" repeated Carol, a puzzled look on her pretty face. "Doesn't one just listen—is it something you have to learn?"

Yes, Carol, it is something you must learn. Good listening is not done just by keeping quiet and having ears wide open. We do not listen just with our hearing, but with our entire being. We must keep thought open to receive ideas just as definitely as we keep ears ready to catch sound.

We learn to listen only as we learn the meaning of absolute quiet, complete silence. For the final reward of listening is the gaining of new thoughts. It would do us little good if the voices of the wilderness spoke to us constantly even though we hear their words, if we had not prepared ourselves to receive mentally those inspirational messages which are the real offerings of nature.

Listening is an art, Carol, it is not a simple little volition. The Bible says, "Study to be quiet." It is a study, yes, a science. Not only must we govern the making of sounds which would interfere with our hearing the still, small voice of nature, we must control all else that hinders our highest sense of hearing. We must cast from our minds the habit of hurry which we have picked up in our rushing, aimless way of living. Nature doesn't hurry, and she cannot make her voice heard by those who do. If we are to be good listeners we must control this hurry habit—which is sort of an illusion anyway. Mere hurry doesn't mean that we get anywhere. Nature always does things on time, moves at amazing speeds, accomplishes marvels—but she does not have that pressure and strain that is characteristic of our hurry.

Carol thought for a moment. Yes! Yes, she could see the truth of these statements. Hurry could keep one from listening. She could feel closer to good listening right then as she let go of the idea that she must hurry.

But that isn't all, Carol. In your young thoughts there may not be as yet place for envy, for jealousy, for resentment, for anger and the other disturbing thoughts that are so often cultivated by all of us if we do not guard against them. But these are noisy thoughts, they rattle in our minds, and we cannot listen while they are there. They block the very things our hearts most want to hear. If we are to know that Sacred Silence, that complete quiet which is vital to listening, we must cast such handicaps from us.

Carol looked a bit startled as we talked of these things.

"And this—this is studying nature, to learn to listen?" she asked, obviously in deep thought.

Yes, Carol, that is where nature study begins— within ourselves, finding, recognizing and cultivating that which is natural in our own thinking.

"Do you know," she added thoughtfully, in a mood that was more calm than we had seen heretofore, "I am not too young to know those things you speak of. I have known jealousy and I guess envy, too—at school, and with my friends. Now that you speak of it I know it was disturbing, it hurt, and I see that I couldn't listen to anything while it was in my mind."

And that morning, before we had taken to a trail or greeted the Sanctuary animals, we three sat on a bench where we could look out over the lake—and we studied to be quiet, to listen.

Carol learned that day that all nature walks with padded feet. The love of stillness is everywhere manifested. Yet silence is not mere soundlessness. There are certain sounds that are noise. There is the boom of a gun, the snarl of a motor, the rattle of traffic, raucous cries that arise merely from excitement—and these are disturbing. But natural sound contributes to silence; it aids listening. Listen, Carol, to the murmur of the pine trees in the wind. Is there anything about that sound which breaks up listening? No—rather it aids our hearing, for it brings peace to our thoughts, helping us to turn away from the annoyances within. Of such effect is the song of birds, the lapping of waves on a shore, the cry of crows and jays, the hoot of an owl. These sounds are the ingredients of true silence; they are hearing aids.

The Indian, who mastered the wilderness without destroying it, was adept at the science of listening. His ear to the ground, to the tree, to the rock on the mountainside, or attuned to the calls and cries of the forest, picked up messages and gathered facts which would have been missed by those less trained in the ways of silence.

Salt and Pepper were wonderful listeners. How often we had watched them on those silent nights when they would be reaching out into distance with their attention! Their tiny little cupped ears were alert, and when something was heard that was of special import, their heads would raise as they studied the soft sounds which reached them.

A deer makes a business of listening. It seems probable that he learns more of the world about him through hearing than he does through sight or smell.

His great ears are built somewhat like the sound-detecting devices used by military forces. They are large, shaped like a deep spoon, and are capable of pointing ahead, to either side, or back. Always they are in motion, turning this way and that, picking up near and far sounds that the deer may know what is going on in the near-by world.

So it is with all creatures of the forest. Their very lives depend upon good listening. They prize silence as nature does. Noise disturbs and frightens them. They are born to a world of quiet; instinctively they know the age-old admonition: "Peace, be still."

That day Carol went far on her way to becoming a good listener. As we hiked over trails she practiced silent steps, avoiding twigs and dry leaves, picking out cushion moss and bare ground to hush her footfalls. She spoke in soft voice or in whispers.

The sun retired in regal splendor that night. The western sky was alight with crimson, while a huge cloud at the horizon was fringed with luminous silver. Shafts of light found their way through openings in the cloud, and reached up into the overhead blue like great beacons.

We found Carol standing in silence looking at this gorgeous display. She smiled as we approached.

"Listening to the sunset, Carol?" I asked.

She laughed. "No doubt there is music in it if we could only hear well enough to catch it," she said. "I never knew there were so many sounds in the world. And I was thinking about this listening business—it isn't just in nature study that you need to be a good listener. You need it among people just as well. We don't really listen often. If we aren't saying something, we are thinking something that interrupts others."

Yes, Carol, listening is almost a lost art in society. Rare indeed is the one who can forget himself long enough to let others speak. Our vanity makes us want to hear our own voice, to have our opinion rule.

"It seems to me I have been here for ages and ages," Carol was saying to Giny. "This is all so homelike, so natural, as if I belonged to it and it belonged to me. These sounds—all so delicate and beautiful—I haven't heard them before, and yet they are familiar."

"You are learning fast," I complimented her. "After dinner we shall test you, we shall find out how much you have learned."

When dinner was over, we put out in the canoe. Stars were sparkling, and a baby moon hung in the western sky.

"What is my test?" asked Carol. "When do I prove to you that I have learned to listen pretty well?"

"The test will come without announcement, Carol," I replied. "If you have lost the noises from within your thoughts, if you have let go of self enough to receive only what the forest world will offer you, you will tell us what we want to know."

We sculled silently along close in to the darkened shore. By agreement we ceased all talking. This was a listening trip. Now we were approaching a place where a little fast-flowing stream enters the lake. Here I let the canoe drift. The voice of the running water spoke softly out of the night.

I watched Carol closely. Soon we would know if she had really let go of her thoughts, and was listening. Giny turned toward me, and I could see her nod her head affirmatively. She was hearing what we wanted Carol to hear. Still we waited. Carol was being tested and did not know it. Suddenly she gave a little start, and looked anxiously toward shore.

"Hear something, Carol?" I asked in a whisper.

She motioned me to silence, and gave her attention to the night. Her excitement grew. She made several little nervous moves that set the canoe to rocking.

"What is it, Carol?" asked Giny.

"I am afraid to say," she replied in suppressed excitement, "but I hear voices of people. There must be dozens of them. Away back in the woods. Is someone lost?"

I laughed quietly, and asked her to listen closely and tell me if she could hear what they were saying. She lapsed into attentive silence again.

"I can't quite catch their words," she said a bit nervously, "but they're there all right. I hear them laugh.

113

It sounded almost as if one said my name. Don't you hear them?"

Yes, Carol, Giny and I hear them. We hear them always at this place on still nights. For these are not people, Carol. They are the Voices of the Woods. It takes a good listener to hear them, one who has forgotten himself. Indians and woodsmen know well the Voices of the Woods; they call them the *Voyageurs* or *Travelers*. They are heard best near rapid water, along the rocky shores of a lake when the waves play in and out of tiny caves, and sometimes they are heard in deep woods when the wind blows but not too strongly. These *Voyageurs* are happy people. Their voices are always filled with laughter. They sing and shout as if going on a picnic. They seem always at the point of saying something you will understand, and yet they never say it plainly. They love to half-pronounce your name. Sometimes they shout like canoeists shooting down a rapids. They seem to come closer, but never do.

What are they? They are simply the sounds of the woods, Carol, perhaps a little stream singing over rocks like the one in the darkness tonight. They are the rustle of leaves, the rubbing of two trees together, the moaning of wind through barren boughs. And when we hear these sounds, in our thoughts we liken them to something in our experience. Thus we think they are voices. Our imaginations enlarge on this thought, and we hear them say our names—almost—and call out definite messages—almost. Those who dwell in the woods know these voices well, and they love them as part of the mysterious beauty of the wilderness. But one must be a good listener to hear them. We do not catch these voices if our thoughts are in a whirlwind of our own making. That was your test, Carol. If you heard these voices of the *Voyageurs* you could not refrain from saying so, and if you heard them, you were listening well!

As we returned to the island, Carol was just about bursting with happiness. We reached the darkened boathouse and started to put the canoe away for the night. Only then did we realize we had forgotten to take a flashlight with us.

"The pier is narrow—don't fall in, Carol," warned Giny.

The answer was *"Splash!"*

Carol was somewhere in the blackened shallow water beside the pier, our only clue to her whereabouts being the squeals, laughs and splashing about which went with her efforts to get out. Reaching down in the darkness, we finally made contact with her upstretched arms, and lifted her to the pier once more. There she stood laughing and giggling, trying vainly to wring the water out of her dripping clothes.

"How on earth did that happen, Carol?" asked Giny, between laughs. "Did you stumble?"

"No!" said Carol, almost in hysterics. "I just stepped

115

backward like this, and went right off the edge——"

And in illustrating it, she lost her balance and fell in again!

There was another wild outburst of squeals and laughter while we pulled the twice-dunked child out. Then we three sat down on the pier so that our immoderate fit of laughter didn't put us all in the water. Memory of silence was gone. The distant shore echoed with our shouts, and for a while we heard nothing but ourselves.

With Giny's help, Carol was finally in dry clothes once more. Seated about the fireplace, we sipped hot cocoa while our laughing tapered off and Carol pleaded vainly for us to promise to tell no one.

It was bedtime, and Carol's eyes were getting heavy. It had been a long, full day for her. But before we retired, we walked down among the trees and stood in silence, for Carol said she wanted to make sure she hadn't forgotten how to listen. We counted the sounds we heard. There was an old bull frog back in a swamp who was singing his bass solo. A cricket was calling. Some creature was wading along in the shallow water on a distant shore—probably it was a deer. Far, far off in the night I could hear the voice of a coyote.

Carol could not quite hear this sound. "What is the sound like?" she asked. "I don't know what to listen for."

I described it as best I could, and we all fell to listening in a most profound way. Carol seemed actually to be straining her ears. There was a moment of intense silence, and then came out in the clear night air—

F-w-e-e-t, f-w-e-e-t, f-w-e-e-t!

"I hear it!" cried Carol. "I hear it—and it seems so close."

It was close, but it wasn't a coyote.

F-w-e-e-t, f-w-e-e-t, f-w-e-e-t came the telltale sound. Soon there was the *sqeak, squeak* of my oars as I headed across the lake to relieve my neighbor of Salt's presence, while Giny told the delighted Carol the story of the whistle. When I arrived, there was Salt on my neighbors' pier *honking* his approval of the ferry service.

117

By the light of a lantern, Carol and Salt were introduced. She stooped down to pet him, but he withdrew a few steps. There he stood looking at her, while she pleaded with him to be friendly. We watched anxiously. Did Carol have the knack of gaining animal friendships? Salt gave us the answer. With several little grunts of decision he walked to her. She stretched a welcoming arm to him. Up he climbed in his most deliberate and self-confident fashion until, seated firmly on her shoulder, he began chewing on her head. Carol had been accepted into Salt's family circle.

IX

PLAY IS THE THING

The Naturalness of Joy

THE next morning we were awakened early by a duet
of Carol's giggles and Salt's grunts. They were both
up before the sun to launch a stanch and lasting friendship. In fact, it seemed to be a case of love at first sight.
Carol kept telling Salt how clever, cunning, and utterly wonderful he was until his masculine vanity was
inflated like a barrage balloon. And Salt couldn't have
given a finer exhibition of showing off had he been an
adolescent youth. He *honked* and *honked* in his
happiest tones. He whirled about like a top, acting
tough. He climbed a few feet up one tree, slid down
and raced to another, climbed a little way on that and
then raced to a third and a fourth, and Carol's rippling
laughter followed him everywhere. He chewed on the
front doorsill, scratched on the screen, then raced
around and repeated the acts at the back door—all to
no other purpose than to show off.

When Carol was called in to breakfast, she was so
exhausted from laughter that she could hardly eat.

"I never knew a porcupine could be so cute," she
said breathlessly. Then in an unsuccessful effort to be-

come serious, she added, "I guess I am not listening so well this morning. But this is so much fun!"

Surely it is fun, Carol. When we speak of silence we do not speak of sadness. Nature wears a smile on her face, for there is joy in her heart.

"Those who do not know the joy side of nature, the actual fun that is found in her creatures, do not know nature at all," I said to her, my own sides aching from laughing at Salt and his antics. "After breakfast I want to show you something about Salt—it has to do with our nature subject for the day."

"And what is our nature subject for today?" Carol giggled some more as she looked through the window to where Salt had gone into a new spasm of *toughness*.

"It is the subject of *joy*—natural joy." And while we completely annihilated the breakfast Giny had prepared, we talked about the good cheer, happiness and actual fun which can be found in nature's creatures.

One springtime, Carol, a pair of tiny house wrens came to our Sanctuary to teach us a lesson we have never forgotten. Jenny and Jimmy Wren, we named them, and they seemed right pleased when they found the little house we had prepared for someone like them. It was a smart-looking house, made of tiny loglets and a weather-tight green shingle roof. It hung from the lowest limb of a hemlock tree not far from our cabin door, for we knew that wrens were sociable creatures. The door of the house was the size and shape of a twenty-five-cent piece, and this was in accordance with their desires, too.

Obviously they liked the house. At first sight of it they made the very air sparkle with their bubbling song. They flew down and inspected the roof—then sang about that. They looked over the doorway, and sang some more. They hopped about the tree in which the house was hung, and found more reason for song.

Now, Carol, a wren has more song per pound than any other living creature. Tiny little mites they are, just about two steps beyond being bugs. But when they sing, a ripple runs all the way from the tips of the tails to the ends of their beaks. The advice is often given to the vocal student, "Put your heart into your singing." A wren goes beyond that. Not only his heart is in it, but all the rest of him, too—even his feathers. He gargles a grand aria!

Nest building began at once, so close at hand we could see every move. While Jenny did most of the work, Jimmy carried on the song. Maybe that means he is lazy, maybe not. Perhaps that song was just as important as the twigs and grass Jenny brought in, and the work she did in weaving them together. Occasionally he would make a contribution of a twig or so, but not often. Most of the time he sat on a small limb above the swinging house and told the world how happy he was. Jenny sang some, too, but she didn't have as much breath for it as he did.

121

The building of the nest went along pretty well. Then through some miscalculation Jenny brought in a good-sized forked twig, too large to be taken easily through the tiny doorway. She tried to force it in, but it stuck. She jerked it out and tried it another way. Again it failed to go through the opening. And now we watched a bit of woodland philosophy we have never forgotten. Obviously Jenny had taken on a task that was nearly too much for her. The twig became lodged in the opening, and she could not budge it either in or out. She fluttered and flew about her task, pushing on the twig and striving to get it through. But hard as the problem was, her happiness was never dampened in the least. Regularly she would deliberately stop her work, hop up in the tree near the swoon-crooning Jimmy, and join in the singing. After a few verses she would return to her task with new strength, and resume her efforts to move the twig. For a long time it defied her. But at the moment when discouragement might have made her give up, she would cease her labors and sing again. Finally between work and song the twig was forced through the little door—and then Jenny and Jimmy really sang! Later, when we cleaned out the house in the autumn, we tried pushing that twig through the tiny door. We found that it took a surprising amount of pressure to force it through. Jenny could never have done it—without a song.

Carol listened delightedly to the story. "I'll bet I know the lesson that teaches," she said.

"What is it, Carol?"

"When you are doing a hard job stop and sing once in a while—that is, keep happy, cheerful."

That is it, Carol. Good cheer is a kind of strength in itself. Whatever the task before us, we will do it better through the power of a happy heart than we will with a heavy one. Nature knows this. In the characters of all her children she has placed a large measure of good cheer, natural joy, a capacity to play. The lives of animals may be severe, yet they are not sad. But their lightheartedness is not light-mindedness. Instinctively they play in a manner that is profitable to them.

Now Salt helped me illustrate this point. Carol stood at the window to watch. I went out to my porcupine pal, and found him in the very mood desired. He was just an imp, ready for any kind of a tussle that might come his way.

Salt had learned to play a game with me. This game, I fear, was often played with time stolen from other things. But he was so cute and clever at it, I could never resist the temptation to indulge. He was not always ready to play. But when he was, as on that morning when Carol was watching, he played with a vigor that made it a lively affair.

It was sort of hide-and-seek. There could be no

question about his understanding the game. He played it with skill, with a spirit of competition, with an appreciation of the objects and aims, and with definite satisfaction when he had *won*—as he always did!

That morning he played in earnest, perhaps conscious of the fair onlookers who watched from the window. As usual the game began with a wild tussle. This was just to stir up proper spirit. He rose on his hind legs and came toward me, waving his front feet, giving a funny little growl as if he meant to eat me alive. I grabbed his paws and quickly turned him on his back, thereby avoiding a quick and rather unpleasant bite which would have been coming to me had I acted with less speed. Animals generally play roughly. They want their games to have an edge on them. A little bit of pain and danger gives sparkle to their fun. Salt was not angry at me, he didn't want to hurt just for the sake of hurting, but he did want me to appreciate his prowess and have respect for his rushes. On his back he grumbled and growled a lot and struggled to get free. I pinched his throat, tickled his tummy, and taunted him. Then I arose and stepped back to give him time to get up. Once more he rushed me, running awkwardly on his hind feet, waving his front paws and growling menacingly. Again I turned him on his back, though this time not so efficiently. He managed to scrape some skin off a knuckle, and in scuffling with him I got two of his quills fastened in my arm.

Now we had worked up to the spirit of the game, and hide-and-seek was on. Salt stood still, knowing what was to happen. I darted away from him and hid behind a bush. He did not follow at once, but waited for the next move of the game. I clapped my hands. This was what he was waiting for. He came at a porcupine gallop in the direction of the sound. After running a few steps, he waited for another sound signal. I clapped my hands, and on he came. This continued until he had found my place of hiding, and there we held another scrimmage like the one with which we had started the game. When it was over, I pulled new quills from my arms, looked helplessly at my wounds, and then suddenly ran away a distance of sixty feet or more, there concealing myself again. Then followed more handclapping, more sound trailing by Salt, and another scrimmage.

This game Salt and I had played in daylight and dark. The routine was always the same. But I always had to quit; he never would. As long as I would continue to hide, he would continue to seek. Sometimes I was a bit unfair. I would not clap when I was supposed to. He depended upon this sound. Since a porcupine does not see very far, he relies on hearing and sense of smell. I was supposed to clap, and he knew it. When I did not, he was plainly disturbed. During the prolonged and unfair silence he might even pass my hiding place behind a tree, bush or building. Then the clapping would come from behind him. How he would whirl around when he heard it, snorting resentfully, and race back to me! After this breach of the rules, the scrimmage which followed would be severe.

Occasionally I would remain silently in my hiding place, not even giving him the delayed clapping. This was not only in violation of the game rules, but called for a retaliatory maneuver. He would listen for a while. Then with sudden realization that he was not going to hear me, he would utter several of his little *honks* and begin searching for my trail. Generally when this had occurred, I had circled silently and arrived at a point from which I could watch him. His triumph was most apparent when he had picked up my scent. Down the trail he would go with his funny little waddle, looking for all the world like a tank that had lost its treads. I could see him following my exact route. And when he caught up with me after this trick of mine, I was in for plenty of trouble.

It was through this latter ruse that I often made my escape from the game—much to Salt's disgust. I would circle the cabin and silently enter the door. He would trail me about faithfully, and when he had run his inquisitive nose against the doorstep and realized he had been tricked, he would fly into a rage. Round and round he would whirl, acting *tough*. He would swing through the brush and small balsam trees as if he intended to knock them down with vicious strokes of his powerful tail. Generally he ended his tantrum by climbing at high speed to the top of a favorite white pine. That was what he did that day as Carol looked on. She was so excited about the whole experience, I thought she was going to climb after him.

"Now, Carol," said I, "tell me what you observed while you were watching Salt play. What did you make of it?"

"Why, he knew rules!" she exclaimed. "He knew what he was supposed to do, and what you were, too. He knew how to play!"

True, Carol, Salt knew how to play. But there is something else we should notice. The things he does in play are such as will develop him, prepare him for his more serious experiences in the forest. In this play he practices his listening. He is cultivating his valuable instinct for locating and identifying things by sound. This same ability will guide him through the woods, it will tell him of approaching enemies, it will aid him in finding a mate. The scrimmages increase his strength, his quickness, his ability to meet problems of combat. Nature is wise with her children. She wants them to play, but in a way that prepares them to meet life's problems.

Later in the day Carol played hide-and-seek with Salt a bit on her own account. But the incidental tussles had to be avoided as being too rough. Yet she saw in her own experience how conscious the creature was of what he was doing, and how earnest he was in it.

That day we spent much time on the trails, looking for the joyous, the play-side of nature. Carol learned, through story and observation, that where there is life there is happiness. Perhaps nature students have made too much of the troubles and tragedies of the forest. No one could be blind to that phase of nature. There are conflicts, fights and problems aplenty among the wood folk. But this is not all there is to be found. If the hours were counted, it would be seen that joy claims the most of them. There is a serious purpose in nature's plans, but she has pleasant ways of accomplishing it.

Carol saw the play of some creatures that day; she heard of others not so easily observed. While we sat quietly at the shore of Vanishing Lake, a great osprey, or fish hawk, circled high, far and wide within the range of our vision. He looked like a great glider, riding the air currents, dipping, diving, banking—in all, having a grand old time! Once men said this bird was always on the hunt, always seeking to kill. But now we know differently. That is not the way he hunts; it is the way he plays. Though he is a predator and lives upon smaller creatures, still his time is not always given to this. He does some things purely for pleasure. And it made his flight more beautiful to us when we knew that now at least he was drawing joy out of a simple experience.

There, too, we watched two red squirrels at play. They were racing wildly along the ground when we saw them, and first thought might be that they were fighting. Such creatures do have their troubles, but this that we were seeing was sport; it was play. Notice, Carol, that the one that seems to be chasing the other never gains on him. They stay the same distance

apart while they race over logs, up trees, through foliage from one tree to another, and circle round and round a great old stump. If this were a fight, one would catch the other, it would not be just a chase. Note, too that they change places occasionally. The pursued becomes the pursuer. Now they have ceased running and sit resting for a moment, only a few feet apart. They comb out their fur with their feet straighten out the ruffled hairs of their tails, scratch a few itchy places—and then the chase begins once more. This is play, Carol.

We saw two fawns at play that afternoon, along an old logging road. Their spotted coats were shining, and they were the very picture of animation. While the beautiful mother nibbled casually at low-hanging leaves, the two youngsters raced wildly about. They took turns chasing each other. Sometimes they reared on their hind feet, striking harmlessly at each other with their sharp front hoofs. Yet notice, Carol, they are never off their guard. In the midst of a playful run, they come to a sharp stop and stand in perfect silence, all .attention. Their large ears pivot this way and that as they listen to the messages of the forest. The wise old mother, too, pauses in her eating to listen, look and sniff around. They know there is danger in the forest, but they are happy and playful in the midst of it. And we have watched full-grown bucks, well along in years, play as do these fawns.

When we first came to the Sanctuary many years ago, there was a colony of otters living up one of the little creeks. They had made for themselves a slide on a clay bank. Human children on a toboggan have no more fun than did these creatures. An otter goes sort of sliding through the world, anyway. He slides along as he travels across country, walking a little and taking advantage of every little knoll to coast. In the winter he slides through tunnels he makes in the snow. He slides into streams where he goes to fish, and so wonderful is he at swimming that he seems to slide right through the water. Hence, young otters (and old ones too) play at sliding. We had watched them often up that little creek. They kept the clay bank moist with water from their bodies. When the fun began, they would back off in the woods and make a run for the slide. Down

it they would go, nose first into the water, where they would dash about giving a demonstration of their swimming which thoroughly outdoes a fish. Then up the bank they would scamper again for another try at it. The competition seemed to be which could get in the most slides. Obviously, the animals were having a wonderful time.

131

Baby beavers at play are most amusing. On the shore of a little wilderness lake in Canada, I once came upon a mother beaver and three youngsters. For a while I could observe them without their detecting my presence. The mother was going about the business of wood-cutting, perhaps for repairing the house or dam, or maybe just for food. The babies went about wood-cutting too, but on a much reduced scale. Their cuttings were about the size of a lead pencil. But they would pick up the little slivers they had cut and carry them along as proudly as if their product was a full-sized dam-making log. Occasionally they would engage in scuffles, rolling over and over and squealing not unlike kittens.

Carol had watched colts and calves, lambs, pigs, puppies and kittens, and laughed at their playful pranks. But she had not known that this spirit was in the wilder creatures as well.

At sunset, after we had eaten dinner, she stood looking at the quiet, colorful beauty of the sky. In soft voice she remarked that it was the most beautiful she had ever seen.

"But the one last night was more brilliant," Giny suggested.

"Yes, I know," said Carol in sweet seriousness, "but everything looks more beautiful since I have found so much joy in the world. Sometimes—" she paused for a moment as if afraid her thoughts might be too serious "—sometimes when you hear all the news reports, it seems as if the whole world is just meanness, fighting. That seems to be all they want to talk about, or write about. And you get the idea that the woods are that way too, with all animals just fighting all the time. Then when you can see and learn that there is fun and happiness and joy here too—well—it just makes everything more beautiful."

The evening was cool. We built a grate fire and sat before it, all three of us a little tired from an active day. But Carol was still ambitious.

"Are we awfully tired?" she asked.

"Tired, but not exhausted, Carol—why? What is on your mind?"

"Do you suppose there would be any chance of seeing Inky if we went to the salt lick?"

We stepped to the door and looked out. The night was marvelously still, trees were dripping with moisture, and mists drifted across the starlit lake.

"It feels like a Magic Night—let's go!" said Giny, who is always ready for forest adventure. While we made our way to the mainland by canoe, she explained to Carol what she meant by a Magic Night, how it was the time when strange and stirring things happened in the woods.

Inky was not at the salt lick when we arrived. We sat in silence for almost an hour, and he did not show up. Perhaps we were wrong about this Magic Night

Maybe something was lacking in it. As we arose to go, Giny, disliking to disappoint Carol about seeing Inky, gave the porcupine call.

Then from directly over our heads, high in a tree against which we had been leaning, came a lazy but friendly answer. *Honk! Honk!* came the call, but it sounded for all the world as if it had come from a grandfather who had been awakened from his sleep and didn't entirely relish the fact. We flashed a light up the tree, and there was Inky. He had been there all the time, but apparently did not think it necessary to come down and visit.

Under our constant pleading he came to life and sluggishly made his way down the tree. Finally he stood, still half asleep, in the midst of the circle we had formed about him. Carol could hardly contain herself.

"So this is the famous Inky!" she said, bending to him. "You funny-looking old fellow. I've read about you, I've seen you in pictures, I've heard about you, but I didn't think I'd ever see you."

Inky looked at her indifferently. So far he was probably reviewing some dream he was having when we awakened him, and if his expression was any guide, he would rather still be dreaming.

At last he took a little interest in things and permitted Carol to pet him. She was amazed at his size, and the great pack of quills he carried.

"You are always having conversations with him,"

she said to me, laughing. "You make him talk—and I wish I could see how he does it."

"Well, now, maybe we can demonstrate," I said. "Just look at him. See how silent, how deep, and how wise he looks. Don't you believe he would have a lot to tell us?"

Yes, she did.

"Well, it seems to me I hear him start to talk now. Just watch him. Anyone could see what he would say if we heard him plainly."

"What would he say?"

"You fellers been busy today?" went Inky's comments.

"Yes, old top, we have been busy. We have been trying to learn something about the way you forest people play, how you know joy."

"Yea! You folks could do with a little information about that." Inky scratched his side, shook out his quills, twitched his nose, and went on. "Sometimes when I hear what you folks do to have a good time, as you call it, I feel sorry for you. Why do you do the things that tear down your health and your characters, and call that fun? Good Balsam Juice, if we animals went carousin' around eatin' and drinkin' things that did us no good, we certainly would be failures at livin' in the woods! You noticed everything you saw in nature was buildin' up, didn't you? You don't find any of our folks playin' around unless that play is makin' him strong and able to get along in the world. That's what play ought to be. You don't have to tear yourselves to pieces just to have fun, do you? We see some human folks go through this woods a-puffin' and blowin' and complainin', hardly able to walk. Lost all their strength tryin' to have a good time. There's so blamed much fun in this world, fun of the right kind —why don't you human beings wake up? Why don't you make your play develop your strength, give you health, spruce up your minds and your characters? Sometimes, by Balsam Juice, I get disgusted with you! You can be so much better and so much happier than you are if you'd only use some common sense."

We all stood in silence. Inky looked from one to another, and Giny stroked his quill-capped head.

"There," he went on, turning to waddle away into the night, "there, I guess I've been too mean again. You folks are kinda sensitive about your faults. You'd rather not hear about them. Rather be let alone even if you're doin' the wrong thing. I suppose I shouldn't talk such stuff to you, even when I know it's right."

Inky was waddling away into the darkness. He took a bite at the salt-lick stump, but wasn't much interested. There was a dream he hadn't quite finished. He reached the base of a hemlock tree and started his climb aloft.

"But remember!" he called back, in his unapologetic

way. "If I've said anything I'm sorry for, I'm glad of it."

"How do you know he said all that?" asked Carol when we had reached the cabin.

"Why, you were right there, Carol," I said, in surprise. "Didn't you catch his words?"

She admitted she didn't.

"Then, young lady, you still have a lot more to learn about listening."

X

THE *SWEETEST* STORY EVER TOLD

The Importance of Right Attitude

THIS was now the third day of Carol's visit to the Sanctuary, and there were two ominous promises written in the morning. Salt had disappeared again, and we knew only too well what that meant! Then there were leaden gray clouds reaching from horizon to horizon. We knew what that meant, too, and we made ready for a rainy day.

In the north country in every season there are days drawn at random from the whole year. There is always the day in spring when autumn winds howl among new-born buds. Temperatures will dip alarmingly low, and we draw close to the grate fire with the feeling that things may have gone into reverse, and winter may be backing up on us. There is a day in every winter when summer pays a surprise visit, a day in every summer when winter returns the call. In autumn there are times when the spring light is so noticeable in the sun that flowers seem half inclined to bloom again and birds recall parts of their songs.

This was one winter day in summer on which we found ourselves faced with a day of cabin confinement.

Gray clouds settled low over the treetops as if to take better aim with their rain. The deluge of drops they released seemed half hardened by the cold wind that whipped them about, scattering them over the forest. Mother birds hovered over precious eggs and delicate

nestlings. Deer crept back under umbrellas of massed cedar trees. Squirrels held to tree-hollow homes. Ground animals sought the dark, damp comfort of their caves, there to snooze the difficult day away.

Giny and I have loved this sort of a fireside day. It brings out the rich joy of hut happiness. But Carol had not yet learned its appeal. At first sight of it she was not too pleased. Her eyes were a bit wistful, her thoughts wishful, as she looked up in vain for a break in the clouds. Nature happiness to her was still symbolized solely by going and doing—she had not found that there is joy in just being. So much had been promised for this day. We were to search the cedar swamp for belated blueberry patches. We were to begin the marking of a new trail. We were to make special pictures of Salt and the chipmunks.

"But Carol, this day is an opportunity!" I said, noticing that she was struggling with a sense of disappointment and frustration. "What a time to write letters, read books, play some music, bake something, rest, and just be lazy."

Carol smiled pleasantly, but she wasn't convinced.

I continued my good-cheer propaganda. "We'll keep that grate fire roaring, Carol, and before the day is done we'll broil bacon over the coals, we'll cook potatoes in the ashes, we'll brew coffee, and we'll pop corn and toast marshmallows. Suppose you learn to bake muffins—Giny will teach you today!"

"That's an idea!" burst out Carol, the sparkle of enthusiasm kindling in her eyes. "I'll bake muffins for dinner. But—" she hesitated for a moment—"will you promise me something?"

I awaited her request, quite sure that the promise would be made.

Carol suddenly became quiet and serious. "Once at a lecture I heard you tell of an experience with a beaver. It was one of the most beautiful adventures I have ever heard. When you were telling it I wished

I might hear it again. But the next time before a camp-fire or grate fire, where I could really feel the scene you described. We will have the grate fire to-night. After dinner, when we are sitting there, would you . . ."

When my promise was given, Carol's spirits rose. Of a sudden the world was abounding with interest and things to do.

When the hour was right, she headed for the mak-ing of those muffins—and ran straight into the arms of calamity! Her first quest was for a large pan in which to mix the dough. She remembered one that had been used for this purpose. The pan was kept on a high shelf on our little back porch. During her short visit Carol had evolved her own way of getting it down from its high perch. She could not reach it, and she did not want to take the time to bring something to stand on. Such methods would have been too conventional for Carol. So she would make a run and jump high in the air, snatching the pan off the shelf before she touched the floor again. It was all wonderful fun and had been a most successful maneuver heretofore. How-ever, it was not so fitting under present conditions. For unknown to Carol, Giny had been making some sim-ple syrup for use in canning, and had left it in this pan. When muffin-making time was at hand, without waiting to ask, Carol ran to the back porch, executed her ballet jump and pulled the pan off the shelf. The weight of the syrup made the pan slip from her fingers. Carol landed on her feet all right, but the pan landed on her head—upside down, fitting like an oversized helmet. The thick syrup flowed all over her, in her hair, down her neck, over her clothes, into her shoes.

Giny and I heard the crash and scream that attended the calamity. We looked through the door, and for a moment were so dumfounded we could not make a move to help poor Carol. The picture we looked on will always remain vivid in our memories. There stood the child in the midst of a sticky, slippery puddle, the pan completely covering her head and neck, the syrup pouring over her as if she were a pancake. Our potential spasm of laughter was held in check for one inquiry.

"Are you hurt, Carol?"

"No!" came her voice from beneath the pan, sounding as if she were talking into a rain barrel. "Not a bit—but I am horribly mortified."

Then while rescue work went forward, laughter shook the cabin. There were rumbles of thunder outdoors as if the clouds were snickering too. Carol, herself, was wonderfully good-humored about it all. I can't imagine anything that would try a disposition more than a syrup bath!

It took several hours of scrubbing before Carol and the entire back porch were restored to order again. When at last things were somewhat normal, and Carol sat before the fire drying her newly washed hair, we asked her if she still felt like making muffins.

"I'll make them if it is the last thing I do!" she replied with a stamp of her foot.

And make them she did! Under Giny's tutelage she did a wonderful job. The muffins fitted well with the ham we broiled in the fireplace, the coffee, vegetables, and dessert Giny had prepared.

As we sat at dinner, looking out at the darkening forest world, the rain still driving in sheets before an erratic and fitful wind, we spoke with gratitude of the sense of home comfort that crept over us. This feeling of contentment was deepened when, with dinner tasks completed, we gathered before the fireplace. Giny sat in a comfortable chair knitting a warm garment that someday would be worn by a soldier in a distant land. Carol sat on the floor at Giny's feet, looking meditatively into the dancing fire. I brought in more wood to keep this home fire burning.

"And now, young man, how about your promise?" asked Carol.

Yes, my promise! We were to repeat the beaver story, which I regard as my most precious wilderness adventure. Not that it excels in excitement or even has the thrilling qualities which the word *adventure* might imply; but rather it uncovers so much about the nature of creation, and implies something of our obligations toward living things.

All right, Carol, you shall have the story. In it we shall find our nature lesson for the day—a lesson which may be summarized in one word: attitude.

It is a fact, Carol, that much depends upon our attitude. This round old world is like a mirror that reflects back to us our own image. If our attitude is right, if there is kindliness in our hearts and in our ways of living, we see that which is kind and beautiful in the world about us. And if the world seems to be filled with meanness, cruelty, and lacking in intelligence, we may be sure that our own thoughts are made up of this pattern. I have not always had adventures like the one with the beaver. This beautiful part of nature was concealed from me for years because I had not learned that the key of kindliness opens the door leading to such experiences.

Some years ago, when I had first learned to love the life of creatures and no longer wished to harm or destroy them, a companion and I were traveling in the Canadian canoe country. Always seeking remote and undisturbed places, we held away from beaten paths and popular routes. We worked our way far beyond the end of the roads, deep into a lake-speckled wilderness.

One day we had made a long and difficult journey. Many portages and miles of paddling lay behind us when in late afternoon we came to the shore of a lovely little unnamed lake. We were so tired we decided to stop there for the night, even though there was no spot very favorable for a camp. We searched around a bit, however, and a little way back from the lake shore among some red pine trees we found a space for our tent.

It is marvelous how quickly a pitched tent becomes home! When we arrived, this spot was just another place in the woods. Now that our tent was there, our sleeping bags inside—it was home! Dinner was hurriedly prepared and eagerly eaten. Then after preparing our camp for the night, we went to bed.

My companion was asleep almost as soon as he had crawled into his sleeping bag. He had a marvelous ability to snore. It seemed to me his eyes could hardly have shut when sounds arose that would suggest a sawmill and a zoo had suddenly been established in that tent—with the saw being fed and the animals not. This was a nightly event in our camp.

I laughed a little at the vocal monkeyshines that were going on. A flying squirrel lighted on the top of our tent, and I followed his path as he scampered across the canvas and went off into the darkness. Through the tent door I could look out into the loveliness of night, and see the silhouettes of trees with stars studding their tangled hair. In mind I was reliving the events of the day, and planning the steps of the morrow.

Then I came to realize that I was in the grip of that strange and wholly enjoyable mood of wakefulness which is known to all men who live in the open. The time comes when there is no such thing as sleep. Forest rangers, naturalists, voyageurs, lonely sheepherders, dwellers of silent and remote places—all know this experience. It isn't insomnia, nor that nervous wakefulness sometimes experienced by those living under the strain of city life. It is simply that life is too full for sleep. Sometimes it seems to be more than that. It is a happy conspiracy in nature to keep the chosen one awake and prepared for adventure.

This experience has come to me often. Sometimes it begins in the middle of the night, sometimes in the early evening; always it holds me under its spell until daybreak. Strangely there is no tired feeling as an aftermath. It is in no way distressing nor exhausting. In the midst of it I have felt as if this were a new way of living in which sleep no longer would be needed. The whole experience is pleasant and desirable.

Hence, when I found myself in the grip of this spell that night on the little Canadian lake, I welcomed it.

I rose, dressed and stepped out of the tent door into the night. Everything in the pulsing ebony mansions about me breathed life, beauty and infinite silence. That is, everything except my companion, who at this time injected some new noises into his snoring, sounding as if the saw had struck some hard knots, and the animals of the zoo were on the verge of starvation.

Looking for quieter surroundings, I moved among

the trees toward the little lake. Starlight was sufficient to outline all things in silhouette. I found a moss-covered log at such distance from the tent as to reduce the snoring to a minimum, and there sat down to enjoy the mystery and loveliness of the forest. The cool night air was a luxury in itself, and I drank deeply of it. Trees dripped with dew.

Through the tree trunks I could look out on the still lake. Its quiet surface looked like polished black marble. In it lay the reflected image of the heavens glorious in mellow starlight.

But even as I watched out over these waters I noted a little disturbance at the far shore. Some creature was starting to swim out into the lake heading in my direction. Whatever it was could be traced by the moving V of its wake, rocking the reflected images of the stars.

I watched closely, realizing that the little disturber of the waters was likely a muskrat or a beaver. I hoped it was the latter because of my deep interest in these animals. I did not definitely identify the creature until it had crossed the lake and stood in the shallows not far from where I was sitting. Then it went through a series of moves that left no doubt. It paused, rose on its hind legs, shook its fur free of water. Then it folded its little front feet to its breast, swaying from side to side, reaching its sensitive nostrils high and testing the atmosphere to see if danger were present. This then was a

147

beaver! Often I had seen these animals do this, so that even in faint starlight I recognized the gesture.

Apparently satisfied with conditions, the little engineer of the wilds began walking slowly into the woods in my direction. I could make out his course plainly, though he seemed more like a moving shadow than something solid and real. After walking a few feet he paused again and went through that silent, patient motion, rising to his hind feet, folding his front feet to his breast, testing the air with his keen nostrils. He came on to within six feet of me where he suddenly stopped, aware of my presence. Here he repeated his act of precaution.

Oh, this was grand adventure! To have this shy little fellow standing there almost within arm's length made me feel that in some involuntary way I had qualified for the confidence of nature. It seemed as if I were no longer an outsider, no longer an intruder, but now one of nature's family trusted with her secrets.

The beaver stood very still, looking intently in my direction. Then two sounds broke out in the solitude which engaged his attention. A loon flew over, so low that the whistle of his wings could be heard. The beaver looked up but showed not the least bit of alarm. An instant later from far, far in the distance came the cry of a wildcat. At this the beaver was all alertness and attention. He faced about in the direction of the cry. Here was the voice of his age-old enemy, the one

of whom he must be most wary. Through long generations while his kind had been living in the forest, building their dams, forming their houses, organizing their
remarkable community life, the wildcat had been a
constant threat, an unending danger. Sometimes a big
beaver has been able to defeat a wildcat in combat, but
usually the victory goes to the latter creature. Hence
the beaver has learned to seek the safety of deep water
when this enemy is at hand. That night I feared the
wildcat cry might bring an end to my adventure. The
beaver stood for several minutes listening into the distance, ready for flight into the lake. But the cry was
not repeated, and finally the beaver lost his concern.
Once more he turned his attention to me.

Then came the climax of the adventure. The beaver
was walking toward me once more. He stopped at my
feet and looked me over carefully, while I sat as still as
I could, though I was trembling with excitement.

Suddenly my little wilderness friend rose on his
hind feet and placed his front feet against my hand,
which was cupped on my knee. He lifted himself up
and looked right into my face, his little twitching nose
so close it nearly touched mine.

I have never been able to describe properly the way
I felt during this experience. There was something
surprising about it, and yet at the time it felt wholly
natural, even though unusual. In that brief moment
there was the feeling that this was reality, this was the

actual nature of things to be seen when we are free of
fear or the wish to kill or harm.

How long the little fellow remained in this position
I do not know. It may have been for several minutes,
perhaps longer. It is rather hard to count time in the
midst of such an event, and I must confess I was about
as excited as I have ever been.

Finally I began to talk to the little creature. It is
well to talk to animals. They may not know the meaning of the words spoken, but I am convinced they know
from the quality of the tones and manner of speech if
they are near a friend or not.

"Hello there, Ameek," I said, using an Indian name
for him. "This is decent of you to come to me in such

a friendly manner, after the way we human beings have treated your people. You are more forgiving than most humans could be, I am sure."

The beaver looked interested and reached his inquisitive nose a little closer. I continued:

"It is a credit to you, old top, a mark of intelligence. And some way I believe you know that I love you and all your fellows of the forest—else you would not trust me this way."

Still he stayed on, turning his head from side to side as though trying to catch every word and to understand. After a time he let himself down to the ground, turned and went unhurriedly toward the lake. He entered the water and swam back by the same route over which he had come. My last sight of him, or rather of the place where he would be, was as he ruffled the waters on the distant shore. No doubt then he disappeared into the woods. Next day I searched the shore looking for his home. But there was no beaver house on that lake. Somewhere in the forest vastness beyond, in a stream or another lake, my little friend lived, but I did not find the place nor did I see him again.

"Are you convinced," said Carol, "that you had this experience because of your attitude—because you had no thought of harming anything?"

Well, Carol, we must be careful in such matters not to get into the realm of mysticism. But I am sure that kindness is not just a mere sentiment. Kindness is a science. It is part of intelligence. It quiets fear, and releases right thinking and acting. One need only look within his own experience to realize that when he is treated kindly by his fellow men he works better, thinks better, serves better, and feels better. This is notably true with animals. There is a fine side of their characters which is concealed by any form of cruelty. Fear floods their thoughts, and they cannot act with their full ability and nobleness. The dogs, cats, horses, and other creatures who live closest to us reveal this fact. One of these animals living under abuse has little opportunity to use his intelligence. Repeatedly it has been seen that animals taken from a place where they are mistreated and moved into an atmosphere of kindness, change in disposition, showing plainly better character and disposition than was before revealed.

So it is with forest creatures. I never saw the native friendship of so-called wild animals when I was a killer of them. I never had experiences like the one with the beaver. It is a fact I accept without question that animals have a way of knowing your attitude toward them. One scientist believes fear in a human being gives off an odor which animals can detect. This odor of fear, he contends, produces fear within the animal, and makes him ferocious. This seems possible, though I could not know its truth. Another thought is that animals may instinctively feel the human attitude toward them. Certainly, even with our crude senses, we feel the attitude of people toward us, know when we are liked and when we are not.

One thing is certain in my experience—when my attitude toward animals changed, their attitude toward me changed, too. Only after I had learned something of the science of kindness did I gain the friendships and wholly enjoyable companionships of such creatures as Inky, Salt and Pepper, Rack and Ruin. I knew I would not harm them, I knew they wouldn't harm me, and they seemed to know all this, too.

The grate fire had burned to coals now, and Carol went about preparing popcorn. Her thoughts still held to the beaver story.

"What you say about attitude—does that apply with people, too?" she asked. She was gathering the very lesson I had planned for her.

Yes, Carol, it does. At a college a professor asked his class to write down quickly the names of people in their personal acquaintance whom they disliked. Some students had difficulty in thinking of any, others could think of one or two, while a few listed a dozen or more. And it was found that those who disliked the most were themselves disliked by the greatest number.

"It seems to be expected of us in this world, Carol," I said, "that we must look for the best, work for the best, believe in the best in order to find the best. That is true in nature, and in man."

The rain continued in torrents. It pattered on the roof of Carol's tent house as she went to bed. And as she bade us good night, she said:

"I am glad we had a rainy day."

None of us had as yet gone to sleep, however, when the expected and dreaded event happened.

F-w-e-e-t, f-w-e-e-t, f-w-e-e-t! The sound came out of the night from the direction of my neighbors' cabin. I tried not to hear it, but it was no use. Again it came.

F-w-e-e-t, f-w-e-e-t, f-w-e-e-t!

Grumbling against the whole tribe of porcupines and their ancestors, I dressed to go on this unwanted errand. Rain seized upon this moment to come down with fresh vigor!

As I passed the tent, flashlight in hand, I heard Carol call to me.

"Is Salt over there?" she asked innocently.

"Yes, he is, the little scamp!"

"Remember now," she cautioned, "keep a right attitude!"

In my thoughts I said, "Aw! Balsam Juice!"

XI

AN ODOR WITH A STRIPE DOWN ITS BACK

A Lesson in Appreciation

THE world was clean next morning after the rain. The forest seemed to have found an extra springtime. Everything appeared refreshed and ready to go again and grow again. The rain-soaked foliage glowed with glorified green. Creatures hurried about as if to make up for the previous day of inactivity. Frail spider webs spread across branches of bushes and low trees, looking as if they might be fingerprints left by forest fairies. Long leaves of red pines wore sparkling gems at their tips—jewels made of drops of water hoarded from the deluge. And everywhere the sun's rays struck they revealed such vibrant beauty that it seemed the whole world might momentarily break forth into song.

Carol was watching the morning. She stood in silence, her gaze resting on one lovely thing after another.

"And what are your thoughts this morning, young lady?" I asked, as Giny and I walked up to her.

She laughed. "It is hard for me to put them into words," she said. "I have been thinking about this rain. I never knew before how important it is, nor how beautiful. Rain always seemed to be something that keeps you from having a good time, something to get your feet wet or spoil a picnic or football game. I didn't realize it is a way of making the world lovelier."

"Learning appreciation, aren't you?" said Giny. "And how much we all need to learn that!"

"Suppose we make that our subject for today," I suggested. "Let's learn to appreciate things by understanding them a bit better."

It was a good idea, agreed Carol. Fine, thought Giny. *Honk! Honk!* said Salt from his perch high in a tree, apparently giving his approval.

"This will be a day on the trails, then," I said, planning aloud. "Let us pack our lunch, fill canteens with water. Get out the binoculars, cameras, the magnifying glass—let's look closer at things than we ever have before, for if we see things well we shall understand them, and if we understand them, we shall appreciate them."

Who was it said that all evil is ignorance, all ignorance evil? This is true. When we understand things of creation we find their worth and beauty, and if we believe they have neither worth nor beauty, we do not understand them.

That day we pried into nooks and corners of nature that were new to Carol. Across our trail went a tiny grass snake. He wriggled his way over the moist rug of leaves, under logs and across beds of moss. We stood watching his remarkable flowing way of traveling. Carol held back.

"It is the only creature I fear a little," she explained, a bit apologetically. "I wish I didn't."

"What is it you fear about them?" I asked.

"Oh, they are cold, clammy—and they wiggle!"

We laughed. Carol would find that most people share her fear of snakes. Yet snakes are not cold and they are not clammy. They wiggle, but surely that is no more threatening than to fly, walk or swim. It is just their way of getting around. Some way this abhorrence of snakes has crept into human thought through the ages, and not many rise above it.

Come, Carol, look more closely at this little fellow who has paused at the foot of a stump and looks up at us, running his forked tongue out and in so rapidly. What is he doing? Merely getting acquainted with the world about him. This is his way of learning things— as the sense of smell is to the wolf, as seeing is to the hawk, as hearing is to the deer. No, he is not poisonous, and he will not harm you. And nowhere in all these northern forests are there any poisonous snakes. The few species that we have are valuable, for they destroy many vermin, keep down the population of insects and small rodents which could become serious pests if there were nothing to control them. These snakes are part of the balance of nature, and they would be sadly missed if they were gone.

Come, Carol, stoop over this tiny green creature. Let go of your fear for just a moment. See his beauty. No bird in all the world is more brilliantly colored than he.

Before our experience with the snake was over, Carol had overcome much of her fear. We had picked him up, held him in our hands, and she had found he was not "cold and clammy." She had watched him wiggle his way along, and had learned what a marvelous way of travel it is. Her final remark probably indicated a complete change of thought about him and his kind.

"Oh, I think he's cute!" she said, and she called a friendly good-by to him as he found his way back into the brush.

That day Carol learned that there is not a creature in all the north woods that is dangerous to human beings. She learned that wolves, wildcats, lynx, bears have their places in nature's scheme, but that they avoid contact with people. She looked through the magnifying glass at little plants hard to see with the unaided eye—the tiny lichens and mosses—and a whole new world of beauty opened to her. With the aid of binoculars she followed the flights of crows, ravens, hawks and eagles, and learned that these birds, too, have a place in nature's plans. We studied everything that came to our attention, thought upon it, endeavored to understand it.

By noon we were a bit tired from our efforts. We

climbed a high hill from which we could see the wooded country for miles around. There we sat eating our lunch and summarizing our experiences.

"Is this the same world that was here last week?" asked Carol, looking about her. "It seems so different to me."

"It is exactly the same world," assured Giny, laughing. "It is always the same, only our thoughts of it change. As we learn to understand it we feel more of its purposes, find more of its beauty, and sense more of its harmony."

It is in getting close to nature that we overcome our ignorance and learn that which makes us see the world in more beautiful light. Nature will not bring our facts to us. We must get out into the world, dip our hands in it, walk along with its creatures, and gather our information as we do berries—from the wildwood itself. Because Carol had that day looked at one snake closely, all snakes were a little less feared, a little better understood. Because we knew Inky, Salt and Pepper intimately, all porcupines were closer, more important. By their friendship, Rack and Ruin had led us to know all raccoons better.

There is a story told of Charles Lamb which illustrates the point. He was walking along with a friend one day, when suddenly he nudged his companion and pointed across the street. "Do you see that man?" he asked. Yes, his friend did. "I hate that fellow," declared Mr. Lamb. His friend was shocked at such words coming from him and asked, "Why? Do you know him?" "No," said Charles Lamb, "if I did know him I couldn't hate him."

It is in our lack of understanding, our ignorance, that our hatred and prejudice are formed—in our appraisal of animals as well as of people.

Now as we sat on the hilltop talking of these things, a passing breeze brought an interruption. It was the pungent, all-pervading odor of a skunk! Giny jumped to her feet, thinking the animal was immediately at hand, though really he was at safe distance. Carol pinched her nose.

"I guess that is wud adibal we wote get close to," she said, speaking as best she could in the circumstances.

"Not right now, at least," I agreed. "But Carol, he is no exception. Did I tell you of our pet skunk, the little fellow that taught us that his kind is all right in spite of their perfume?"

"Do you diddut," said Carol, hanging on to her nose. "I'd lige to hear id if I cad lissed this way."

"All right," said I laughing, "listen as you please. I think this story will give you a better idea of a skunk than you will get just from his odor."

Some years ago, on a silent August night, a companion and I were standing still in the darkened forest back of the Sanctuary cabin. We heard some little animal moving around near us, though we paid no attention to it at first. It would be strange indeed if something were not prowling around constantly at the Sanctuary. The little something-or-other circled about us, rustling leaves and occasionally cracking small twigs. We felt little concern until it came up and sniffed at our very feet. Then we thought it time to investigate. Especially were we puzzled about that *sniff*—it was quite a different *sniff* from that of the contemporary pets. So a flashlight was brought into play. The beam revealed a skunk standing between us, though my friend and I were barely three feet apart!

Now a skunk is not the offending, obnoxious creature people generally think him to be. He is not just "a bad odor with a white stripe down its back." That nose-curling, eye-watering odor of his is his defense, and nothing else. It is a perfect defense, to be sure! But he does not use it unless annoyed or attacked. It is a fluid contained in a sac located at the base of his tail, and is forced out in a spray or stream by muscular contraction. The fluid itself can be expelled only to a distance of eight or ten feet, but playful little breezes love to pick up the scent, carrying it far and wide, making every living thing that has a nose wish it didn't have— for the time at least. Yet the creature itself is not aggressive, not anxious to be unpleasant. He simply puts new emphasis on the first rule man should know in dealing with wild life: "Let us alone, and we will let you alone."

However, I am always anxious that a skunk fully understand I *am* letting him alone. I want no misunderstanding. That was the way my companion and I felt that night at the Sanctuary. Here was this little striped beauty so close either of us could have touched him simply by stooping. He was unexcited and unafraid. We certainly wanted to keep him that way. We stood so still we hardly ventured to breathe.

But our little friend showed not the least evidence of alarm. And he does have such evidence, which it is well to know. If annoyed, he will first chatter his teeth, an act which says in substance, "Mister, I don't mean you any harm, and for your sake more than mine I hope you don't mean any for me either!" When his teeth begin their chatter, it is well to give him a wide berth, though there are two other warnings given before calamity comes. Next he will stamp and scratch the ground with his front feet. This move is a bit more ominous and says, "Now mister—I am trying to tell you what is best for your own good. You're asking for trouble. Well, you'll get it if you don't watch out! Don't come any closer, or else——" This advice is quite good, and there has been many a suit of clothes lost to mankind because it was not followed soon enough. The skunk is not anxious for trouble, is patient, but those who stay beyond this second warning had better be nimble-footed. The skunk will slowly raise his tail, and hesitate for just one short moment. This is the last chance, you tormentor whatever or whoever you are. Run! Jump! Fly! Climb a tree! Call a taxicab! Do something and do it quickly! For in this move the skunk says, "I hate to do this, but you're asking for it. Maybe you're just ignorant. Maybe you don't know that I am complete master of some four hundred square feet about the place where I stand!" He still hesitates, but one more move on the part of his foolish opponent, one thing that convinces him that he is really threatened, and there will come that stream or spray of yellowish fluid which brings dismay and defeat to all his enemies. It is shot with amazing accuracy at any angle, and woe be unto the creature within its range!

While the results of this deluge of perfume are seldom serious, still the experience is sufficient to change the plans of any animal in the forest. The battle is over when the skunk has declared himself. There is no second attack by him, nor on him. If it is an animal that has been so foolish, it is probably rolling around on the ground trying vainly to rid itself of its troubles. If it is a man who has been on the receiving end, he is a social outcast for some time to come.

That night our friend bore us no ill-will, and we were quite anxious not to create any. We stood very still while he sniffed about us—once rising and placing his front paws on my knee. I dropped several peanuts near him, from a stock carried in my pocket, but he was not interested. When he had moved a few feet away so

163

that I felt safe in doing so, I went into the cabin and brought some bread for him.

"Here, Halitosis," I called, as I tossed a slice to him—and thereby he was named!

He accepted the bread with enthusiasm. He did not mind in the least if we walked about him. No doubt he had been coming to our feeding station for some time without giving us a chance to see him. Probably he had cultivated a taste for bread by sharing that left out for raccoons, and likely he had absorbed some of the confidence common to animals at the Sanctuary.

After eating several slices of bread, he moved slowly into the darkness.

"Come again, Halitosis," my companion called after him, and Halitosis did.

We saw more and more of him in the days that followed. He developed such confidence that he would come to us on a trail. He took bread from our fingers, and loved to have us scratch his head. Once we coaxed him into the kitchen and fed him there. But we never did that again! During his stay a pan fell from a hook, making a startling noise. Halitosis went through all three of his warnings in record time. He chattered his teeth, stamped his feet and raised his tail almost simultaneously. Fortunately he stopped there, though we tremble to think what might have happened had another pan fallen at that moment.

For two years we had the friendship of this interesting, useful and really beautiful creature. He remembered us from season to season. In those two years only once did he use that defensive and offensive odor of his. Even then, we had to admit it was justified.

We have a rule at the Sanctuary that no dogs come there. We love dogs, and someday hope to have one raised in the spirit of the place so that he will live at peace with the forest creatures. But strange dogs would hardly understand. It was a strange dog that caused Halitosis to break his fine record of nonbelligerence.

It all happened one eventful day when Butch, a fox terrier, beautified by a recent bath, was brought to the Sanctuary by his two masters, a man and his wife. We were all out on a trail at the time they came up to our pier in their launch. Not knowing of our ruling about dogs, they landed, released their pampered pet, and all went strolling about the near-by trails. While the two people admired the beauties of nature, Butch had a wonderful time chasing chipmunks and squirrels.

All was well for a time. Then suddenly all three of

the visitors, woman, man and dog, stopped short and stared at something a few feet ahead of them in the trail. There stood Halitosis, looking upon them with interest and not a little challenge. Who were these strangers that had come to his domain, and what was that funny-looking animal who acted as if he owned the whole earth?

The people stood still and that was wise. But Butch didn't and that was foolish. Perhaps hoping to be a hero in the eyes of his masters, he advanced toward the innocent-looking kitty, barking his loudest. Away off in the woods we heard those barks. We started back to the cabin, but arrived too late. In the meantime Butch came on toward this stubborn creature who dared stand still and defy him. The two people called commands for the dog to come back, but in vain. Halitosis chattered his teeth. *Butch came on.* Halitosis beat the ground with his front feet. *Butch came on,* barking his egotism. Halitosis raised his tail. But Butch only barked the more furiously, and approached closer. Then, oh, then!—the air between the two animals was suddenly filled with a fine, yellowish mist that centered upon the dog. Butch turned a somersault backward. He was totally unprepared for this chemical warfare. Bewildered, surprised, dismayed, his egotism completely deflated, he coughed and sneezed violently and rolled about on the ground. His masters turned and made an inglorious but wise retreat. Halitosis waddled slowly away as if nothing had happened.

When we arrived, we looked upon a strange sight. Obviously Butch had been a close companion with his masters. With childlike trust he had always run to them whenever hungry or in trouble. Now he was in trouble, plenty of it, and he wanted his masters. Hence he ran to them, or at least toward them. But for some reason he could not understand, he was not so welcome as usual. His masters ran away, Butch after them. This was the spectacle we saw as we came over the last ridge and looked at the scene of battle. Two people racing frantically through the brush calling to Butch to go away, Butch following just as frantically yipping at the top of his voice.

Comprehending the situation (the atmosphere still bearing record of what had happened), we produced an old blanket. Through our combined efforts the disillusioned and trembling Butch was caught and wrapped in it. His distressed masters took the dog home, there to struggle with the problem of making him sweet and savory again. They called back that they would return the blanket, but we implored them not to. Just bury it, we said.

As they left, Halitosis was standing on a little knoll, calmly and unresentfully watching them. In a letter that came from these people later, bearing an apology, they referred to him as "that awful animal." But I never told Halitosis about this. He wasn't mad at anyone, and went right on befriending the human race by eating harmful bugs, beetles, grubs, rats and mice, and I did not want him to think this service was not appreciated.

While I told this story, the summer breeze continued to bring us strong messages from the skunk somewhere in the brush. Carol had let go of her nose, saying, "I suppose even his odor isn't so bad, when you have learned to appreciate him."

"Whew!" said I, grabbing my own nose and pinching violently, as a fresh blast of skunk greeting came upon us. "It dodt bake eddy differedse to be how dice he is—he sbells jusd as bad."

"I udderstad whad you bead," agreed Giny.

Our hilltop seemed to be a good place to leave at that time. We took to the trails again and filled the afternoon with continued efforts at appreciating our world.

Evening brought a happy surprise. Friends who live near the Sanctuary, who know the forest well and love it deeply, came to call on us. We all gathered about a campfire, choosing a point on our island where we could watch the fading afterglow in the west and the rising evening star in the east.

There is good medicine in a campfire—medicine that heals our mixed-up thoughts and gets us into step with the universe. Perhaps it is because the campfire has in its history a record of security as well as warmth. Wilderness travelers have always gathered about it, finding its warm rays like protecting arms. Our fire gave us that feeling of security that night. Its golden glow played upon the trunks of pine trees, set grotesque shadows to dancing in the surrounding woods, and lighted the faces of those who sat in the circle. Smiles are a bit brighter about a campfire, laughter a bit more merry. Songs are more sincere when accompanied by the crackle of burning cedar; friendships seem more dear.

I took Carol out in the canoe a short distance from the island, so that she could look back on the scene. This is an experience every lover of beauty should have.

When we returned to the circle, conversation had taken a happy trend. Each one was asked to tell a nature story from his own experience, a story that would fit into our thought of appreciation. A forester told something of how trees serve the human race, how they have given us shelter through the ages. This green brotherhood we call the forest holds the earth in place with its roots, holds the rain for use in dry seasons, mellows the heat of summer and the cold of winter, and by its deposit of leaves helps build the very soil in which grows our food. From trees come the lumber for our homes, ships and factories. They give us paper on which to record our news and knowledge, chemicals for our industries. The coal we burn is but the trees of earlier ages. In their spacious branches nest the birds. In the cool and quiet of their groves tired men have found rest. Indeed, the list of their blessings seemed endless. Another member of the circle told of the invaluable service the earthworm does in its treatment of our soil. And there were stories, all true, of dogs that had saved human lives, of horses in amazing bits of devotion and intelligence. Salt joined the party, uninvited, and *honked* along with the general conversation, perhaps saying he had experience with human beings, and while they could improve, they weren't so bad. But one story in particular we shall all remember. It was a remarkable adventure with a loon, the experience of our friends who told it.

One day in early winter, these friends were returning to their home, having made a trip to the near-by town. The first crystalline beauty of winter rested upon the forest, and lakes were closed over with newly formed ice. It was on one of these lakes that they discovered some living creature, obviously in trouble. Closer investigation revealed that it was a loon. The bird was trying to fly, but could not get under way. For a loon is so big and heavy, his wings so relatively small, that he cannot rise into the air unless he is on water. He must gain his primary momentum from rapid swimming, coupled with motion of his wings, and only after he has gone a considerable distance in this manner will he be able to take off. Hence, on land he is helpless, either to fly or walk. He casts himself forward, slides on his breast, and crawls along in a most awkward and original fashion.

This creature had made some miscalculation in landing on that lake. Perhaps something was wrong with him, and he had to land. Or maybe the new ice, still clear, looked like water to him. Anyway, there he was on a flat, hard surface, from which he could not rise.

At considerable risk to themselves, my friends went out on the thin ice to rescue the bird. At first he fought with them, but they succeeded in throwing a coat over him and bringing him to shore. His great size amazed them. They pondered some method of getting him into the air, but knowing the limitations of such birds, they took him home to care for him. Some frozen fish were obtained for him, and with the offer of this food, his attitude changed at once toward his benefactors. The fish was cut up in strips, that he swallowed whole. He seemed to understand immediately that no one would harm him, and with abandon and much awkwardness he tried to climb in the lap of the one feeding him. He was so comical in his actions that he was named on the spot—"Ludy, the Ludicrous Loon."

If Ludy had searched the country over, he could not have found for himself a better home. Two tubs were put at his service, one filled with water, where he could, and did, splash around at will; the other filled with blankets, to serve as a nest. When he was first placed in his tub-nest, he did not take to it, but cast himself out and made away as fast as he could. He paused, seemed to think better of his action, and immediately returned, jumping into his man-made home. From then on it was his! He understood it that way, he liked it, and he returned to it whenever he sought rest or refuge.

There was a big old cat in that home, and at first the people were concerned as to his idea about the big bird. The two creatures eyed each other thoroughly, apparently decided everything was all right, and thereafter were friends. Once the people witnessed a little event which gave them momentary alarm. Ludy's tubs had been placed in the basement. The people saw the cat go through the open basement door and down the steps. Looking after him, they saw him make a sudden jump into the tub-nest where Ludy was resting. They fancied he was attacking the bird, and ran to the rescue. But on arriving, they saw the cat emerge with a good-sized rat in his mouth. They never suspected the cat after this.

Ludy was much loved in that home, and he was devoted to his human friends, too. Yet he would tolerate no strangers to come near him, nor did he want his friends to be close if they were wearing clothes that were new to him. He ate about three pounds of fish daily. Only one part of the experience bore the least unpleasantness to these people, and that was Ludy's constant calling. Long had they loved this sound out of doors. But when it was uttered in the house, it reached a new and distressing melancholy pitch. It seemed a bit different from other loon calls, too. There was more loneliness in it, as if in thought he were reaching out for his wild freedom, or calling to some mate who could not answer.

When real cold weather came, Ludy was moved up into the kitchen, tubs and all. Here he found new pleasures that he loved. He was closer to his human family, for whom he was developing a deep affection. Particularly did he like the evening gatherings about the fireplace. As the family finished its activity of the day, and drew chairs before the fire, from the kitchen would come a violent *thump!* No one was concerned, for it was just Ludy getting out of his tub-nest. Then there would be a series of *thumps* as the great bird waddled and hobbled his way awkwardly into the living room. Right up into the family circle he would come, murmuring his happiness, and settling close to one he loved in particular who would unceasingly pet him. He would stay there through the evening, until the warmth of the fire had made him sleepy, when without ceremony he would return, sliding, slipping, flopping, falling back to the tub, and retire for the night.

Ludy came in November. It was the hope of his friends that they could care for him until spring when the lakes would open again, and he could live naturally. But one night in late February Ludy went to sleep and did not awaken again. Perhaps he arose on wings we could not see, calling anew in tones we could not hear, into a land that welcomed his free, wilderness-loving spirit.

At any rate, Ludy lived to teach us anew the beauty of animal character, and to learn himself that there are human beings who love and appreciate living things. For now, when we hear the weird cries of this strange creature, we think not in terms of "a crazy bird," but of the intelligence and friendliness we know is there.

A campfire party ends slowly. In fact, it is difficult to tell the exact moment when it ceases to be. Our fire burned low until it was only a bed of glowing coals. Our friends paddled unhurriedly away in their canoes, calling and singing back to us from far out in the darkness. We sang bits of the evening songs as we walked to the cabin. Giny made a discovery.

"Why, Carol dear, you are crying!" she exclaimed, hurrying to the child who stood looking out a window. Big tears were coursing down her cheeks, but immediately we knew they were not from sadness, for there was a smile playing about just back of them.

"I don't know what else to do!" said Carol. "I tried laughing, and singing, and talking, but none of them tells enough."

We understood. One has sensed little of the real beauty of the natural world if he has not been moved to tears.

XII

W–O–R–R–R–K, W–O–R–R–R–K, W–O–R–R–R–K

Industry and Intelligence

THE fifth day of Carol's stay at the Sanctuary started with a *bang*. That is no mere figure of speech. It was a *bang* that echoed and re-echoed about the silent, dark-draped shores of the lake. The clock was counting off the first hours of a new day, and we all were sleeping peacefully when suddenly at the very side of our cabin there came a startling *crash,* followed by scrapings, bumpings, and the noisy flight of an empty can down the hillside. The disturbance shook the forest out of its slumber, set the squirrels to chattering, drew questioning twitters from sleepy robins, and brought a snort of alarm from a deer on the mainland.

"What's that?" called Carol from her tent house. We echoed her question.

Honk! Honk! Honk! said an innocent-sounding voice somewhere overhead.

"There's your answer!" I called to Carol, and then to the invisible porcupine, "Salt, you imp, what in the world have you done now!"

He *honked* some sort of an explanation as I dressed

176

and went out to investigate. His tones were soft and sort of saccharine sweet. He reminded me of a youngster who has spilled a jar of jam all over everything, and then tried to avoid punishment by acting like an infant angel. I heard him scratching his way down a tree trunk, and he fairly cooed his greeting as I walked up to him.

"Yes, Tom Sawyer," I snapped, "mighty innocent, aren't you? You don't fool me with your sweetness. The only reason I don't give you a whipping is because I don't know how it could be done."

It wasn't difficult to see what had happened. A ladder had been left leaning at a sharp angle against this tree, a few feet from the cabin. Salt, with his fine knack of doing disturbing things, had chosen that particular tree for a nocturnal climb. Hundreds of trees around, but he had to pick that one! As he climbed upward, no doubt he had wedged himself under the ladder, forcing it outward until it tipped over. The ladder had crashed against the house, scraped and bumped its way to the ground where it struck an empty kerosene can and sent it bouncing along on a noisy downhill journey.

The first gray streaks of dawn were spreading along the eastern horizon as I stood there scolding my porcupine. Giny and Carol were laughing. The whole Sanctuary seemed very much awake.

Salt took my scolding as high praise. He came hustling down the tree and right up to my feet—wanting to play! While I continued telling him what I thought of any four-footed rascal that would break into our sleep and stir up the whole north woods like that— he whirled about *honking* happily and acting all too cute. Before I knew it we were caught up in an energetic session of hide-and-seek.

Soon Carol had dressed and joined in the game. The two of us bewildered poor Salt by hiding in separate places and clapping our hands simultaneously. He did not know which way to go.

Now Giny had dressed and had come to watch the fun—and to sympathize with Salt because of our unfairness. Salt was trying his best to play in accordance with the rules. We would have our preliminary tussle as usual. Then he would stand still while I ran to hide. When I clapped my hands, he would start toward my hiding place. But then suddenly Carol, hiding in an opposite direction, would clap her hands. Around Salt would whirl, and race or waddle toward her. Then I would clap my hands—then Carol—then I— then Carol—until Salt was dizzy from jerking his head around. Finally, disgusted with such flagrant violations of the rules, he climbed a tree, grunting his opinion of us, which I dare say was not too complimentary.

Then the forest quieted down once more, and we three stood there looking at the cool loveliness of dawn, listening to the first bird songs. In the eastern sky ribbon-like clouds were touched with pink. Little puffs of breezes were moving about through the trees which bent stiffly as if they were doing their morning exercises.

"The world is getting ready to go to work," I said. "Maybe we should get an early start. Today we are going to study intelligence and industry as we find it in nature. What do you two say? The sleep is out of us now—shall we get out in our canoe and start searching?"

The three of us agreed it was a good idea. At once we were animated with plans and purposes. Giny would prepare a bite of breakfast. I would get the canoe in the water.

"Let me get the canoe ready," pleaded Carol. "I know how now."

"All right, Carol," I agreed, knowing the canoe was light enough for her to handle. "I'll get some wood, then."

Each went about his chosen task. But it wasn't more than three minutes until we heard a scream and a splash at the pier, and then laughter.

"Oh—she's done it again!" cried Giny with amused concern.

I hurried to the scene of the commotion to find that our suspicions were true. Carol *had* done it again! She was just climbing out of the water onto the pier as I arrived. Obviously she wasn't hurt.

"Good Balsam Juice, how did that happen, Carol?" I exclaimed as I ran to help her. She was laughing so she could not reply at first. Finally she managed to explain that after she had got the canoe into the water, she stepped into it, only to find herself suddenly deposited into the lake. It was all so quick, she couldn't understand how it happened.

"Well, I know what you did," I said with conviction. "You must learn how to get in a canoe. There is a little trick to it. Are you too cold, or do you want to learn right now?"

She wasn't cold, she said, and in fact she enjoyed her morning dip.

"Well, it will only take a minute. Now watch me," I said, pulling the canoe alongside the dock with a paddle. "You cannot just step into a canoe, for the action of stepping pushes the light craft away. That is how you got into trouble. You walked into the canoe, the canoe jumped away—and you know the rest from experience. Now observe closely...."

And in slow motion I demonstrated the accepted way of getting into a canoe. "First get the canoe closely alongside the pier," I explained, matching my words with actions. "See that all paddles are out of the way so you won't step on them or stumble over them. Then balance your weight on one foot, and reach out with the other to the center of the canoe. Do not step out, just reach out. Now note when my foot touches the right spot in the center, I just *shift* my weight from the foot that is on shore to the one in the canoe. This prevents pushing the canoe away. When my weight is shifted to the canoe, I lift my foot from the pier—again without pushing, and see, I am safely in the canoe without even rocking it."

"I think I understand," said Carol, watching closely, her clothes dripping a pool of water. "Would you do it once more?—and then I'll try."

"All right," said I, beginning the repetition of words and actions. "Now notice—the canoe is alongside the pier. All paddles are out of the way. Now, I balance myself on one foot while I reach out to the center of the canoe with the other. You see I have not *stepped* into the canoe. My weight is still on the foot on the

181

dock. That makes it impossible for me to push the canoe away, or lose my balance . . ."

All of which sounded very logical, and looked reasonable—until the foot on which I was so "safely balanced" slipped in some of the water flowing from Carol's clothes and I went gliding into water waist-deep!

For a moment Carol stood speechless. Seizing upon her silence, I tried to pretend this was all in the instruction.

"And you see what happens, Carol, if I do not watch my footing," I said in matter-of-fact tones. "It would have been wiser for me to pick out a dry spot to stand on. And furthermore . . ."

But I got no further. Carol could not be deceived longer. This feet-first dive of mine had not been intentional and she knew it. She doubled up with laughter, and her squeals brought an anxious inquiry from Giny as to what was going on. We falsified that everything was all right, each one hesitating to tell on the other. I climbed out on the pier, sputtering something about our next lesson including instructions for getting out of a lake.

Giny had finished breakfast preparations. Morning light was growing and the best canoeing time slipping past. She came out of the cabin door to call us—and then stood gasping at what she saw. There Carol and I stood side by side, our clothes soaked, our shoes gushing with water, our expression somewhat like that worn by Salt in his innocent pretensions.

"Now how in the world did this happen!" asked Giny.

"Oh," I said casually, "I have been showing Carol the right way to get in a canoe."

"He's a fine, thorough teacher," said Carol in mock seriousness.

"And she's a most apt pupil!" I commented.

Giny threw up her hands in helplessness.

The sun was tipping the pine trees with red by the time we had changed to dry clothes, eaten our breakfast and were ready to go. We got into the canoe while I received many a jibe about my mishap. We moved silently over the waters, gliding through banks of gray mist. In a tall birch tree along the island shore Salt was busy eating leaves. We thanked him for awakening us to such a world of lively beauty, but he never looked up from his eating.

It felt to my paddle as if the canoe were coasting downhill that morning, so easily did it glide through the reflections and among the pillars of rising mists. Despite our hilarious moments before our departure, we sat in silence now. The canoe sang a little song as its bow gently ruffled the waters.

"Where to?" asked Carol, in a soft voice.

Anywhere would have been all right. The world

was sparkling with miracles, and we could not have picked out a direction that did not lead to interest and adventure.

But there were definite plans in mind. "We go to the Bay of the Beavers, Carol," I said, "for remember we are to look for intelligence and industry in nature. Where better could we find it than in the life and work of the beaver?"

And we talked of the tremendous activity we looked upon in the natural world about us. Quiet it was, to be sure, but *active*. Everything in the universe was moving, developing, growing, working ceaselessly at its evolution. Nature will not have it otherwise. Creation is based upon energy. Work is a law which cannot be broken. Never does anything stand still. Even while a clock ticks a single second, everything that exists has changed a little, moved a little, grown or developed a little. Plants have their plans to follow. Animals find in their instincts a demanding design for their lives. Rocks and rivers, lakes and lands, are in ceaseless motion. Mountains are building up and wearing down, continents rising and falling, waters are forever rising in evaporation, raining upon the earth, and racing in rivers back to the sea. Every star in the heavens is on the move at staggering speed. The universe is set in motion, and in motion it must remain.

"That is why we all must learn to work, Carol," I said, as we were nearing Beaver Bay. "Laziness and idleness are against the grain of nature, and they bring no happiness. It is the busy individual who is in step with the universe. The lives of all successful men tell us that there is no real rest but action, no joy in life except in well-directed work."

But our conversation was silenced as we noticed an animal swimming through the smooth surface of the water. We had now entered Beaver Bay. Paddling stopped and the canoe drifted on silently. The little swimmer who had caught our attention passed within a few yards of us. It was a beaver and he was towing along a freshly cut aspen limb about two feet long and four inches in thickness. No doubt he was headed for the large beaver house that looked like a great pile of brush on the shore back of a protecting point of land. This house was being enlarged, strengthened and prepared for winter. The small log the animal was taking in would find its place among scores of others similar to it.

As the beaver disappeared into misty distance, we noted beneath us on the bottom of the lake a great cache of food his clan had gathered for the winter. It was a large pile of leafy brush cut from live trees, and weighted to the bottom by stones and water-soaked logs. When the lake was frozen over, these animals would swim under the ice and feed upon the bark of the twigs and branches.

We sculled in close to shore to see the work that was

being done. A large number of trees had been cut. Most of them were aspens, though a few white birch, cherry, black ash and maple trees had been taken too. Looking from this one point where our canoe touched the shore we could count twenty-five trees that had been cut down by these energetic little workers. These trees had fallen in all directions of the compass. There is a story widely spread that beavers can drop a tree in any direction they wish. If this is true, their wishes are certainly many and varied. My observation leads me to the conviction that not only do they let the chips fall where they may—but the trees as well. Certainly, in that little patch on Beaver Bay there was no evidence of directional cutting. The trees before us were this way and that, lying uphill and down, and across each other in a way that would be most inconvenient for the further work of the beavers. It seems reasonable that the little creatures would not want them that way if they could prevent it.

Now we heard a gnawing sound not unlike Salt's *crunching* at our doorsill. I turned the canoe in the direction of the sound. Cautioning Giny and Carol to be silent, I poled the canoe along, careful that my paddle did not create even a whispering whirlpool. We were dealing with a creature who is the touch-me-not of the forest. If a sound, a smell, a little motion caught his attention, he would be gone.

The gnawing sound increased in volume as we

neared its source. A bit of brush at the shore gave us some concealment as we approached. And there a few feet back from the water we saw a fine old beaver working earnestly at an aspen. The tree was fully eight inches in diameter, and he had cut it nearly half through before we arrived. The animal was so engrossed in what he was doing that he did not notice us. He was a good-sized beaver, weighing about forty pounds. The ground about him was strewn with chips from the tree. Some of them were five, six and seven inches in length.

Now he was showing us just how this cutting was done. He stood upright on his hind feet, braced firmly by his flat tail, his front paws against the tree. With

his chisel-like amber-colored teeth he cut deeply into the wood, then quickly cut in again about five inches lower. Then he bit into the wood midway between the two cuts and pried out a big chip. This he dropped to the ground. Now he cut out another chip and yet another, until he had chewed his way almost through the tree. Occasionally he would cease his labors, move back a few feet, and survey the tree as if determining just when it would fall. Then he would return to his task and the chips would fly again.

It seemed to us as we sat there watching this little drama of nature that we did so by special privilege. The forest had opened a secret door for us and we had tiptoed in. But we knew we were there on probation. One breach in good manners, one move that would break and profane the silence, and our adventure would be closed. We were guests, spectators, and must behave as such.

But the busy old beaver continued his work. The chips he was cutting out were not so large as heretofore. He was working more at the center of the wound he was making in the tree. Presently the tree bent a little to one side. There was a crackling sound as the last bit of supporting fiber commenced to break. The beaver moved quickly. Retreating a few feet for safety, he beat upon the ground with his flat tail. This seems to be a warning to other beavers that a tree is to fall. It is their way of saying, "Timber-r-r!" The tree now came crashing to the ground. Strangely, the sound made not the slightest disturbance among forest folk. There was no break in the bird songs. There was no saucy chatter from a squirrel or snort from a deer. The old beaver himself made no move. This was a natural, expected sound. The wilderness had known such events through the ages.

But our composure was at an end. Carol, carried away by what she had seen, turned about in her seat at the canoe bow to join her enthusiasm with ours. The canoe rocked until it dipped water.

"Carol!" called Giny, in a voice that was not so subdued as it was intended to be.

"Carol!" I called, striving to steady the craft, barely catching my paddle as it was slipping into the lake.

"Sorry!" whispered the excited Carol. But her apology was not enough for the beaver world. Within a few feet of our canoe there came a sharp sound as if someone had struck the water with a flat board. Immediately it was repeated. It sounded like a muffled gunshot. Another beaver had been swimming silently, looking us over. When our moment of excitement came, he simply warned the forest there were intruders present. This warning is given by the beaver striking the water with his flat tail while he makes a quick dive. It is a startling sound, and while it has a special message for beaver people, all creatures of the woods will become alert and cautious.

The beaver that had been doing the cutting lost no time in seeking safety in the lake. Soon there were two of them swimming about, getting farther and farther from the scene, repeating their crash dives all the while.

No need for us to be cautious now. The show was over. Those beavers would not return into the presence of such discourteous guests as we had proved to be. Besides, the sun was now high in the morning sky, and these little creatures prefer not to be about in daylight.

We laughed freely. I presume Giny and Carol did not know how near we had come to another swim that eventful morning. When a canoe tilts far enough to dip up water, it is all too close to going over. But here we were right side up and dry, so why worry?

Since we could see the beavers no more, we landed and took a look at their work. The freshly cut tree lay on the ground near its rounded stump, on which the teeth marks of the beaver were plainly etched. This tree would now be cut up into convenient lengths of from two to three feet each. In nights to come the cutting would be done, and at each place where a cut was made there would be left on the ground a pile of chips. The smaller limbs would be used for food. Some of them no doubt would be taken to the food cache we had seen on the bottom of the lake. Larger pieces would be towed away and used in construction of the house.

We were amazed at the number of trees the beavers had cut. Scores of them lay along the shore.

"There must be a hundred beavers working here!" exclaimed Carol.

"Probably not more than six," I corrected, for the work even a single beaver can do is always difficult to comprehend.

We walked along the shore to their house. It lay in a well-chosen spot near the water. The little workers had heaped it high with newly cut wood. As winter approached they would plaster it with mud mixed with leaves and grass. This material in among the sticks and small logs would form a sort of reinforced concrete. Inside this structure the animals would live in well-made, ventilated rooms, safe from all natural enemies. The entrance would be one or more tunnels running up from the bottom of the lake.

Our morning adventure had begun a long and busy day for Carol. By nightfall we were all pleasantly tired. But we had come to understand anew what it meant to be "busy as a beaver." We had seen how they cut roadways through the forest, clearing out brush, logs and stones, so that they can drag materials to the lake shore. We saw canals that had been cut far back into the woods, in which they could float their cuttings. And we had visited a stream in which they had built a dam, creating a fair-sized lake.

It was in the building of this remarkable dam that the beaver showed best his energy and intelligence. The dam has a definite purpose. In streams where there is a fairly constant flow of water the year around, or in lakes where the water level remains somewhat the same, he seems satisfied with conditions. Here he will build his house on the bank or shore, making no effort to construct a dam. Such was the case at the beaver house we had seen that early morning. Beavers building homes in that way are generally referred to as lake beavers or bank beavers. But this creature must have water of fair depth the year round. Hence, in streams where the flow is slight or rapidly changing, he finds it best to create a pool or lake of his own, and he builds a dam. Thus by good engineering he can keep the water near the level that suits him best.

The pool which he creates serves in many ways. It gives him water deep enough so that he can dive and escape from his enemies such as the wildcat, coyote, wolf, lynx or panther. The depth of the water prevents the pond from freezing solid, and enables him to store food on the bottom. And by keeping the water level from rising too high or dropping too low, he may build his house so the floors of the rooms in which he lives will always be several inches above the surface.

Beaver dams are never built twice alike, for the conditions surrounding each site chosen would be somewhat different. Sometimes beavers perform remarkable engineering feats in constructing them. There are cases on record where they have dammed streams wherein men had previously failed. Always their construction work is strong and well-suited to the place selected. The lengths of these dams vary considerably. Some are only about twenty feet long; generally they will measure sixty to one hundred feet, while one in Yellowstone National Park has an overall length of approximately seven hundred feet! Hundreds of tons of material were used in the construction of this remarkable dam, and a good-sized lake has been created by the backwater.

But no less remarkable are their well-planned canals. These ditches are dug deliberately to serve the beavers in their problems. They run from the beaver lake or pond back into the forest, sometimes for great distances. Generally one to two hundred feet of length will bring the canal to the place desired, but there are records of great ones over a thousand feet long, six to nine feet wide, and having an average depth of water of nearly two feet! Through the canals the clever little creature may swim and tow logs and branches from distant groves of trees. Here, too, they may feel greater safety from their enemies. The beaver is at a disadvantage on land when a wolf or wildcat approaches, but once in the water, he is well able to take care of himself.

It is probably because he is so intelligent that many weird stories have been written about him. When pioneers were first pushing west from the Atlantic seaboard, they seemed to be in competition to see who could tell the biggest beaver stories. Of course, they were thinking much of beavers in those days. It was the seeking of beaver furs more than all else that caused people to penetrate the western wilderness. In colonial days, beaver skins were a kind of currency. Fortunes were made out of their fur; wars were fought over preferred trapping grounds.

Then it was that such stories began as that of a beaver using his tail as a trowel in building his home and dam! It was said, and believed, that he actually drives stakes with his tail! He has a remarkable tail—but not that remarkable! He does use it as a rudder when he is swimming. He uses it in his crash dives, as we have already seen, giving warning to wilderness creatures. He braces himself with his tail when he is cutting a tree. He thumps the ground with it when a tree begins to fall. But there have been too many tall tales told about beaver tails!

Just think—a beaver has no tools to work with except his teeth, claws and his remarkable tail! Yet he builds a house of forest materials! He constructs a dam perhaps hundreds of feet long! He cuts trees of considerable size, the largest on record being a cottonwood forty-two inches in diameter! He digs canals, calculating the slope of land and flow of water!

His ability to work—his inherent industry—fully matches his intelligence. No doubt that is because there could be no true intelligence *without* industry. The two are one—and laziness is a form of ignorance. The beaver is not fanatical. He does not always work, but when there is something important to be done, he puts his heart, soul, teeth, claws—yes, and his tail, into it.

During summertime he shows his humanness again. He takes a vacation! He and his family may go on a trip, traveling miles and miles away from their own home. But as autumn approaches they are back, getting ready for winter. It is then that we look upon such industry as to make us exclaim in admiration.

Imagine the amount of effort, the number of trips it takes for them to cut and bring in the great volume of material used in their house and dam. Think of the scooping, dragging, biting of roots, and moving of stones necessary to prepare one of their canals! And their community appears to be a true democracy. Every beaver works, young, old, male, female, each anxiously doing his share. There is no boss, no dictator. There is no prison or penalty necessary, for each one wants to do his part!

A little incident in the history of a northern lumber company shows something of the beaver's determination and his ability to work.

This company was putting in a narrow-gauge railroad in preparation for a certain logging operation. In surveying the course of the road, they came to a stream at a point where a beaver dam had created a wide pond. This presented them with something of a problem. Building long bridges is an expensive thing, and

195

they wished to avoid it if possible. The men had a choice of two things: either they could change the course of their railroad and cross the stream below the dam where a small bridge would suffice; or they could (they believed!) tear out the beaver dam, let the water out of the pond, and bridge the stream thus narrowed where they were.

They chose the latter course—unfortunately for them! In accordance with this plan, one day they tore out a large section of the beaver dam, and went away to give the pond a chance to drain. They calculated that by the next day the water would be so low that they could begin work on their bridge. But when they returned the next morning, they found that the beavers had fully repaired the dam during the night. There it stood stronger than ever, reinforced with new material, and the water of the pond just as it had been! Determined, the men tore the dam out again, making a much larger break than before. They would show these little "flat tails" who was boss. But again, during the night, the beavers did a wonderful repair job—and the dam was in perfect condition by the next morning. This time the men became rather violent. They blew up the dam with dynamite. The beavers built it up again. The men tore it out again, however, and believing a far-spread story that beavers are afraid of a light, they drove a stake in the center of the newly made break, and hung a lantern on it! They returned in the morning, confident that this time they had outwitted their four-footed competitors.

But what a sight met their eyes! There was the dam, fully rebuilt, higher and wider, and the lantern, still burning, sat on top of it. The *flat tails,* far from being afraid of the light, had built their new dam right up underneath the lantern, so high that the bottom of the lantern·actually rested on it! After that the lumbermen changed the route of their logging road, and crossed the stream at another place. This happened in the early logging days, but even now one may see the bend in that railroad right-of-way, where men had to alter their plans because of the undefeatable industry of beavers!

While beavers are sociable among their kind and generally live in colonies or communities, it happens occasionally that one will draw away from beaver society and live by himself, even as a human hermit. There are many guesses why they do this. One thought is that such solitary creatures have lost their mates and prefer to live alone. Another is that they are lazy ones, or perhaps outlaws, and are driven away by their fellows. No one knows the true explanation, for we cannot read the thoughts of the beavers.

There is the story of one of these solitary old beavers, living alone in a backwoods pool, who took a dislike to trout fishermen. There were trout in his pond, and he did not want those fish disturbed. He simply abhorred fishermen. Other people could come to his home without fishing equipment, and he would pay no attention to them. But let someone start casting a fly around and the old fellow would swim wildly about the surface, beating the water with his tail and frightening the wily trout. While that beaver lived, no trout were caught in that pond. It wasn't that the beaver wanted the fish for himself. Beavers do not eat fish or any other kind of meat. But apparently he liked the companionship of fish, and he had his own way of protecting them.

As the day was closing, Carol, Giny and I stood upon a beaver dam in a forest creek back of the Sanctuary. Before us lay the little lake created by the backwaters. Dead trees and bushes stood in the water in great numbers. And in the deepest part of the pond was the beaver house. Tiny streams of water were finding their way over the top of the dam, making little musical waterfalls whose songs fit well into the wilderness.

Years ago I had watched this dam built. The creek was rather a tiny one, not more than ten feet wide. However, the beavers had found it to their liking. There was a constant flow of water, and the banks of the stream were lined with fine groves of aspens. The little engineers set to work, and it was most interesting to watch them. First they felled a number of trees and cut them up in sections to get material ready. Then they took small live branches and began forcing them into the stand at the bottom of the creek at a chosen point. I did not understand the purpose of this at first, but soon it was clear what they were doing. They continued placing these branches at this point until there was a row of them from bank to bank directly across the current. It made sort of a picket fence through which the creek waters were filtering. It was now that the beavers revealed their plan. Upstream from this newly made fence there were several places in the creek where there were deep holes. In these, through the years, there had accumulated a deposit of decayed leaves, grass and mud on the bottom. The wise little animals deliberately dived and stirred up this deposit, scratching it and digging it loose, until the creek was filled with floating material. As the debris drifted down, it came against the fence they had prepared and was caught there. The little fellows kept stirring up more and more of it in the stream above, and sending it drifting down. Finally enough of it had been caught at their fence for the flow of the stream to be held back—and the first step in the building of their dam had been successfully completed. Now they brought in the newly cut logs and placed them in proper position. Then layers and layers of mud and leaves were added, until a dam twenty feet long and three feet high had been made. This had created a pond large and deep enough for their winter needs. Year after year the dam was enlarged until it was over three hundred feet in length.

"It is wonderful!" declared Carol as the significance of her day's experience was dawning upon her. "But isn't this a great waste—I mean in the trees they cut and destroy?"

Yes, Carol, there is some waste from our human viewpoint. Throughout the ages beavers have been in the forest doing as they do today, and in general they are beneficial to the woods. But where we human beings enter the picture some of their work is damaging. There are instances where beavers have cut down a farmer's fruit trees, and where their ponds have flooded valuable tracts of timberland. In such cases they must be removed.

Yet they are friendly to the forest. Their ponds hold back the water deposited by spring rains and prevent it from rushing down streams, causing floods and carrying away fertile soil. In dry seasons winds blowing across these ponds carry moisture out to near-by plants and trees. Ducks and other water birds find their ponds fine nesting places. In many cases beaver pools are a great benefit to fish life, and they are effective in combating forest fires. But their greatest contribution to the growth of the forest comes over a long period of years. As hundreds and hundreds of their pools accumulate decaying leaves, logs, grasses, lily pads, mud, etc., they are building up fertile soil for the future. In our mid-western states many millions of acres of our finest forest and farm land have been created by prehistoric beaver ponds. Thus they have been serving us for ages. It is one of nature's most effective ways of building up soil. And today the beaver ponds of our northern forests are doing this work, making lands where the finest trees of the future will grow.

When evening had come, we guided our canoe into Beaver Bay once more to see if our little furred friends were continuing their labors. Moonlight was strong and the landscape lighted with a soft glow. Small birch trees at the shore line looked like fairy fingers pointing to the sky. Pine trees made grotesque, clown-like figures with their silhouettes.

Now we heard the familiar gnawing sound as a beaver chewed patiently and persistently at a tree.

"Do you know what he is saying?" asked Carol in a whisper.

We awaited her answer to her own question.

"He says *w-o-r-r-k, w-o-r-r-r-k, w-o-r-r-r-k!*" and her impersonation of the sound was so fitting, Giny and I whispered, "Good!"

We sat for some time staring toward the shore whence came the sound, our canoe drifting among lily pads that reflected the moon. Suddenly Carol drew our attention in another direction. With a silent wave of her arm she pointed on down the shore line. We looked, and the sight we saw drew a whispered exclamation of wonder and admiration. There at the water's edge stood an enormous deer, still as a statue, studying the night. He looked more like some great, graceful spirit than a flesh and blood animal. I risked a whispered comment:

"Giny and Carol! That is the Antlered King! He is the largest buck in all these forests!"

It was hardly necessary to speak of his size. Other deer we were seeing regularly would have been dwarfed beside him. Probably he weighed nearly four hundred pounds. This was the great creature who had left his tracks along the sands and the trails. It was he whom we were always so anxious to see and whom we seldom looked upon.

He bent his great antlered head to the waters and bit off a lily pad. Then he raised up again and stood looking about alertly as he chewed his delectable bite. As yet he had not noticed us. No doubt we were hidden in the shore-line shadows cast by the moon. Then the grand old creature, a monarch among his people no doubt, began walking slowly in the shallow waters. With each step he raised his leg high, as if on parade. We scarcely breathed, so thrilled were we by this wilderness picture.

But suddenly close to our canoe there was a sharp sound like a muffled gunshot. Our beaver friend had discovered us, and executed his sound of alarm by slapping the water with his tail and diving. We might have been more startled had it not been for the magnificent action of the Antlered King. He bolted upright on his hind feet, his front feet pawing the air in the manner of a spirited horse, his great head bent far back. Still on his hind legs, he turned majestically toward land and executed a graceful leap into the shore shadows. By the sound of breaking brush we could trace his flight through the black forest. Then the wildwood settled back to silence again, except for the occasional splash of the beaver now far out in the lake.

"Good Balsam Juice!" ejaculated Carol, for want of something better to say. We were all so completely under the spell of our adventure that any comment seemed inadequate. We just sat looking at that place in the curtain of night where the Antlered King had disappeared. Finally Giny made a suggestion of which we all approved:

"Let's not talk about this now—just keep the picture in our thoughts," she said in a half whisper. "Suppose we go home and to bed in silence. This adventure will be ready for conversation in the morning. It is too precious for words now."

W-o-r-r-r-k, w-o-r-r-r-k, w-o-r-r-r-k, w-o-r-r-r-k began anew the song of the beaver as we paddled back to the cabin.

XIII

CAROL FINDS HERSELF

Individual Responsibility—Nature's Plan

THERE were three things demanding our attention when we awakened on the morning of Carol's sixth day at the Sanctuary.

First, the weather had made one of those quick changes characteristic of the north country. The wind was whipping out of the north. Across the sky clouds of gray with dark undersides went scurrying, looking like flocks of frightened sheep. We heard the wind whistling through our window screen before we were out of bed, and we knew it was a day for heavier clothes, stirring activity, hot soup and grate fires.

Our next discovery was that Salt was gone again. The bread left out for him on the doorstep had not been touched, and the island had that empty feeling. Well might our neighbor start practicing with his whistle—and I might as well get ready for a hurry call just at the most inopportune time. It wouldn't be long before Salt would demand the accustomed ferry service.

But our first two discoveries of the morning were quickly forgotten in the third one. Carol was gone too! She did not respond to our calls. Giny hurried to her tent house. Everything was in good order, but Carol was very much absent. A note was pinned to her pillow, and Giny brought it to me.

"Gone to Vanishing Lake," it read in hurriedly written script. "Hope I see a bear. Don't wait breakfast for me, please. Love, Carol."

"Should she have gone alone?" asked Giny, a little concerned. "Do you suppose she can follow that trail?"

"I would rather she hadn't gone," I replied, for I knew that though the wilderness will not hurt you, there are many ways to hurt yourself in the wilderness. "However, that trail is quite plain and she's been over it a number of times. If she doesn't return reasonably soon, we'll search for her."

I went to the pier and found that Carol had taken a rowboat. On the mainland I could see the boat at the shore where she had landed to take the trail.

Time tries to be mean on occasions. When there is anxiety present it likes to drag along. That is the way it seemed this morning. The few minutes we were straightening up the cabin and getting our breakfast seemed hours long. Continually we were looking toward the mainland, hoping to see Carol and her rowboat heading for the island. We called loudly, but the high wind just caught up our voices and swallowed them.

It was blowing a gale now. Trees were bending low before the pressure of the wind, and across the lake marched legions of white-capped waves. Clouds charged along barely over the treetops, and there were brief showers of hard-driven cold rain. This was a typical north-woods day, the kind that gives character to the country. On such a day one feels the rigor of the wilderness, the power and wildness of it. There is a challenge in it. It dares the nature lover to come out, and when he responds it puts the color of health in his cheeks, and brings to him a rugged happiness that is not possible in nature's milder moods.

Normally we love well this sort of challenging day. But with Carol alone in the forest and probably not properly dressed for such conditions, we were much concerned.

We could wait no longer. It was time to begin the search. We packed some food and dry clothing in a packsack, and in our canoe crossed the now foaming waters to the mainland. Leaving the canoe on the shore near Carol's boat, we walked at a stiff pace down Vanishing Lake Trail.

"If only she doesn't get frightened!" I said, as we hurried along. "Nothing will harm her unless she loses her head."

"And we must not get frightened for her," cautioned Giny, noting my mounting concern.

I smiled and slackened my pace which had become almost a run. Certainly this was a time for clear and calm thought. "Thanks!" I said, though I was finding it far easier to be unafraid about myself than it was about someone else. Many times I had been in the forest not knowing just where I was. The thought of fear had never come to me for I knew well nothing in the woods would harm me, and I knew I would figure out my problem sooner or later. In fact, I have always found a large measure of genuine pleasure in being lost. There is something of a contest in the circumstance, and it gives a feeling of intimacy with the forest. But to think of Carol who was new to the woods out there alone on this kind of a day was taxing my composure.

Vanishing Lake Trail offered no evidence that Carol had been over it. The intermittent showers of rain had washed away any tracks that might have been there. We called continually, but our voices were muted by the roar of the wind. Trees were lashing back and forth now and occasionally we could hear a crash as one of them, unable to stand the strain, fell to the ground.

Carol was not at Vanishing Lake, and there was no evidence that she had been there. The little spruce trees along the shore were bending stiffly in the gale, and the small lake was staging a sort of toylike storm all its own. High overhead two eagles were having a grand time riding the wind. How we wished that we might have their wings for a few moments to rise and look about the country! It was a futile feeling that confronted us. We could not see, shout or hear beyond a range of a few yards. Carol might well have been just over the next ridge and we could not have found her nor could she have known of our presence.

But there was nothing to do but keep searching, small as was the area we could observe. We took up

each little side trail, climbed hill after hill, shouted until we were hoarse, but all we heard was the voice of the wind.

Hour after hour went by and our search continued. There was a growing seriousness to the situation that we could not deny. Darkness would be coming all too soon. We needed help at once if Carol was to be saved from spending a night in the woods. Two of us were not enough to search effectively such a vast territory. The forest rangers must be notified and a searching party organized.

We returned over Vanishing Lake Trail to our

canoe, and then to the cabin. To reach the ranger's station we must cross a long stretch of rough water to the place where our car was stored, and then drive seven miles over a forest road. An ax must be taken along, for it was very possible that trees might have been blown across the road. Before beginning this journey I changed to dry clothes and made ready for long hours in the forest. Rain had ceased for the time, but the wild wind blew stronger than ever. Poor Carol —of all days in the year she would have to be lost on this one!

I had left the cabin to begin my journey alone, Giny remaining to receive Carol in case the child succeeded in returning by herself. As I walked toward the pier I heard a tiny sound that suggested the squeak of some distant gate. I called to Giny to help me listen. Even above the gale we heard the sound again. No question about it, there was something in the air other than the many voices of the wind.

And it wasn't the squeak of a gate!

F-w-e-e-t, f-w-e-e-et, f-w-e-e-t, came the unwelcome but commanding whistle from my neighbors' cabin.

"Oh, no!" cried Giny. "Not that, at a time like this. Salt can wait this once."

But the whistle insisted, *f-w-e-e-t, f-w-e-e-t, f-w-e-e-t,* and then it gave a series of short quick toots that certainly indicated a desperate state of affairs. Surely the language of that whistle was such as demanded response.

"I'll have to go," I said resignedly. "I can do it quickly. But what do you suppose that porcupine has done now? Probably chewed the back door off their cabin, or maybe he has eaten his way right down through the roof!"

While the insistent whistle continued its commanding message, I got into a boat and rowed over hill after hill of high waves. I was so busy at the oars I seldom looked ahead, knowing well the course to my neighbors' pier. As I neared shore where I was protected somewhat from the wind, I heard the expected.

Honk, honk, honk, honk.

I answered back in porcupine language.

Again came the *honk, honk, honk*—but this time it was followed by an outburst of merry laughter. Now Salt can do many things that surprise me, but he couldn't do that! I turned quickly in my seat to find Carol standing there, buried deeply in the folds of a much oversized rain coat.

"*Honk, honk, honk,*" she was calling, along with laughter. "I'll bet I look like a porcupine at that."

My own joy at seeing her could not be restrained. Standing up in the boat and beating my breast in Tarzan fashion I gave the old north-woods war whoop, which is reserved for such exultant moments. *Wa-a-a-ho-o-o!* The sound bounded down the shores even above the roar of the wind. Giny heard it, and with the aid of the binoculars learned what was happening.

"Carol, you blessed child!" I exclaimed with what breath I had left. "How in the world did you get here?"

"She came out of the woods," my neighbor was calling from his half-opened door. "Just the way that pesky porky comes. And if you would just as soon, we would much rather she keep coming than he. She doesn't chew our doorsill and she doesn't scratch on the screen!"

"They were so nice to me," Carol was saying, as we got into the boat and rowed away. "They took me in before their fire and cooked a hot lunch for me. I don't blame Salt for liking to go there."

Carol looked about as bedraggled as when I had fished her out of the lake on her all too numerous duckings. Her hair was twisted about like tangled rope, and her clothes, somewhat dried by our neighbors' fire, were a nondescript pattern of wrinkles and mud.

"But Carol," I said, much puzzled, "how did you get there? That is a long way from Vanishing Lake. There are swamps and swamps, and no trails that lead that way."

It was too windy to carry on much conversation as we crossed the lake, and our reunion was too joyous and noisy for explanations immediately. However, in the

14—T.M.S.P.

course of time, we got Carol's version of her experience. She had followed the trail to Vanishing Lake all right, going out just about dawn. There hadn't been much wind when she had started, just enough to make the forest talk mysteriously. She had seen several rabbits as she hiked along. There was a porcupine in a tree and she had called to it, hoping it might be Inky, or perhaps the long-missing Pepper, but she had received no response. There was a deer drinking at Vanishing Lake, and of course this must be Bobette, she insisted. And there was a long little animal, built like a dachs-

hund, that darted the length of a fallen log not ten feet from her.

"A weasel, Carol," I said.

It was a cute weasel, then, insisted Carol. The creature had paused for just a moment and looked at her in rather friendly manner before he disappeared in the brush.

But beautiful as was the experience, she had begun

thinking of breakfast. She ate some malted milk tablets she had brought along, but they were an unsatisfactory substitute for bacon and eggs, or perhaps Giny's special pancakes. She rose to return to the cabin, but decided to take another trail.

"Another trail?" I questioned. "Why, Carol, there isn't another trail."

"But I found one," she declared. "It was a small one and wound around a lot, but I could follow it—at least for a way."

Carol, Carol, Carol! That was a deer trail. Yes, a deer trail. These animals have their paths through the forest, and for generations they go over the same route. Their tiny hoofs wear a deep rut, and the trail becomes as well defined as if it were made by human feet. However, it is well not to follow their paths, for deer do not necessarily wish to go where we do, so their trails may well lead us astray.

"That is just what this one did," agreed Carol, her eyes dancing with excitement at recalling the adventure. "It circled around hillsides, and sometimes there were several branches. I always took the one that seemed to be most used."

Carol had followed the trail without knowing what direction it was taking, until she found herself on the margin of a tangled swamp. The trail was quickly lost in crisscrossed logs, moss and massed cedar trees. She realized she could not get through. So she turned about and went back to the top of a little hill, and there sat on a comfortable log to think things out. From here she could see beyond the swamp. She decided to circle the swamp on the high land, and pick up the trail on the other side. It took her some time to do this, really longer than she had figured, but at last she came upon a well-defined trail again. Then suddenly she realized she was standing beside the very log on which she had been resting before she started this maneuver. She had circled the swamp completely without finding another trail, and had at last returned to her starting place.

Then for a few moments she was frightened. The realization came that she was lost. Now the first rain was falling, and she had brought along only a light jacket. The wind was increasing, and she said the whole woods were saying *boo* at her. She had been wanting to see a bear; now she was afraid she would see one. And she confessed that there were a few tears flowing.

"But I tried to remember all that you have taught me," she said. The adventure was all joy now. "I remembered that there wasn't anything in the woods that would hurt me. I remembered that you said we must learn to be quiet. And I sat right there and prayed until I felt all calm inside. Something happened within me. I——"

Carol paused for a moment, as if seeking a way to explain something that was hard to put in words.

But she brushed past the matter, declaring that she wasn't afraid any more. She started to figure things out. She declared over and over again that she could solve that problem. She recalled that Vanishing Lake was west of the cabin, therefore if she went east she would come to the shore of our lake. But which way was east? There was no sun to give her the slightest hint. She tried to recall some of the woodcraft stunts she had read in outdoor books. There was something about moss growing on the north side of a tree, but when she looked at the trees near her, the moss was about even all around. Just as well she hadn't trusted that one. Like most of the storybook woodcraft, this sign is unreliable. On the south side of a hill, where there are few trees and the sun can shine on their trunks, the moss would grow thickest on the north side of the trees, since it likes shade. But conditions make this undependable. Only one sign Carol could have relied upon had she known it. The topmost branch of an uninjured hemlock tree points east. But one must know a hemlock tree, and must be sure it is uninjured before one can trust that pointing finger. If the sun were shining, she might have pointed the hour hand of her watch toward the sun. Halfway between the hour hand and the shortest distance to twelve o'clock would have been approximately south.

But Carol had figured out something that was of greater help under the prevailing conditions. It occurred to her that as she had walked back to Vanishing Lake the wind was striking her right side. Hence, if she walked now so that it struck her left side all the while, she would be retracing her steps. She adopted this course and held to it.

"Fine thinking, Carol," I complimented her. "Excellently done. You were fortunate that the wind didn't change, though."

She realized this, but felt certain such a strong wind would not change suddenly. From then on her story was one of travel difficulties. She had continued on her wind-directed course regardless of obstacles. Sometimes she was in swamps, sometimes in dense brush-filled areas, sometimes among tall pines where the walking was relatively easy. She remembered the caution against hurry, and walked at an easy pace, resting when tired. Several times she had stopped to call, but realized her voice would not carry far. Finally she came to the shore of the lake not far from our neighbors' cabin.

"And do you know," she said, still quivering with excitement at her adventure, "I was a little bit sorry when I found out where I was. It had been grand working it all out, and . . ."

Again she paused for want of words. For a moment her eyes became distant, and her lips relaxed in a strong smile.

I felt as if there were something very vital in her

story which we were not getting. This child had had an adventure deeply impressive and with an edge of danger to it. She hadn't just blundered through it, she had *thought* her way through it. Great things happen to people in times like that.

"Carol," said I, "do you remember what thoughts came to you when you sat on that hill? I mean, just before you got the idea of letting the wind guide you back. Was there something that impressed you a great deal?"

Carol flashed a look at me that was almost reticent. The smile died from her lips, but there was an expression in her eyes that was rich with deep feeling.

"Yes . . ." she said, but again she hesitated.

"Can you tell us?" asked Giny, drawing her chair nearer and taking the child's hand in hers.

"I wonder if I can," said Carol. We sat in silence as she tested her thoughts and searched for a way to express them.

"You see, when I first realized I was lost, I felt pretty helpless," she said. "Always I had had someone to ask about problems, someone to figure them out. But now there was no one. I told you I prayed. I prayed long and hard. Then for a few moments I just sat there quietly looking around. A strange feeling crept over me. I realized I wasn't the only one that was lost. Some part of all those who love me was lost, too—you people, my parents, my friends. If anything happened to me, it would hurt everyone. I shouldn't have gone alone on that trail. I knew it. It wasn't fair to you. And I knew I had to get out of the woods not only because of myself but because of everyone. I felt . . ."

"Responsible?" I suggested.

"That's it—I felt responsible. I simply had to win. I prayed some more—and while I was praying, the last bit of fear left me. It was the strangest feeling. I knew that I was all right and that I could do the right thing. I was so sure of it I laughed at the rain as it beat in my face. When the wind blew hard I dared it to blow harder, and it seemed to me . . ."

She hesitated again and bit her lip.

"You won't laugh at me, will you?" she asked.

"Of course not," I assured her. "We are grateful if you will share your experience fully with us. We are learning something by this."

"Well," she continued, "it seemed to me that this wasn't being lost at all. I actually felt as if I had been lost all my life, and this experience was finding myself. I was directly in touch with real things. There was no one else to turn to, to solve things for me, and I was dealing with nature firsthand. Do you know what I mean?"

We knew very well what she meant. Who has not stood at that glorious moment when it seems that God Himself has called him by name and directed him to do an important task?

"It seemed to me," Carol was saying, "that there was no more important thing in the world to be done than for me to get out of that woods. And what made me happy was that I was the only one who could do it. It was my job. I just knew I could do it, and now—" she gave a delighted little laugh—"now I know I can do anything that——"

"—that God asks you to do." Giny finished the sentence to Carol's satisfaction.

And so, Carol, in your hours in the woods, trying though they may have seemed, you saw that great truth which all nature reflects and which we must all understand. It is *individual responsibility.* Nature grows, evolves on that plan.

Here about us lies that great forest, useful, beautiful, a boon to the whole earth. But it was only a good forest because every tree in it was being the finest tree that could grow where it grew. Every tree and shrub was giving its all to growing; nature would accept no less. No tree could wait upon its neighbor; it could not say, "If others will grow, I will too—otherwise I won't." Nature works on the perfection of the individual. And because each tree was doing its best, accepting full responsibility for living, doing and growing with all its power, the forest is strong and beautiful.

Nothing that lives is excused from this law of nature. Every creature is being the best one of his kind that he can be. He is solving his problems, arising to conditions.

Even the common grass blade, or the lowly dandelion is forever devoting all its power to growth—being the best plant of its kind that could grow, where it grows. This is the principle on which the universe is built.

Evening came early. The wind moderated somewhat but still blew at a lively pace through the gathering darkness, playing a strong symphony on the pines. Daytime clouds broke their solid array, and soon stars were peeking between their dark forms. The moon rose and plated the fluffier ones with silver.

The day had been filled with so much thought that Carol felt we should see wise old Inky before bedtime. We paddled to the mainland accordingly and started toward the salt lick. But long before we had reached Inky's realm, we came upon a good-sized porcupine in the middle of our trail. The creature was not in the least disturbed by our presence, or our inquisitive flashlight. Obviously it was not large enough to be old Inky. Yet it showed definite interest in us. Giny gave the little porcupine call. The animal answered.

"Do you suppose it is Pepper?" asked Giny, excitedly, and she continued calling the porky in its own language.

The creature answered again. It raised on its hind feet and shook out its quills. Then with sudden abandon it began whirling about in a dance of *toughness*.

"It *is* Pepper!" cried Giny, as the three of us moved

forward toward the happy creature. And then it made a move that removed all doubt. Breaking out of its whirling dance, it made a dash for me, wrapped all four feet about my leg and bit sharply into my knee. That was Pepper's old stunt. A wild porcupine would never do that. This was our pet who had now been absent for over three months.

At the cost of half a dozen quills imbedded in my hand, I took the enthusiastic animal from my leg and tussled her about on the ground. She always had been rough in her play, and her long life in the woods had not made her any more gentle. For a few minutes we had a right lively time keeping her overcordial and affectionate greeting from scarring us for life. Then she literally danced her way off into the dark brush, as if to say she was glad to see a little of us, but didn't want too much.

The three of us stood laughing and calling after her for some time. It was good to know for certain that she was still around, and had not forgotten us.

We moved on to the salt lick. The cake of salt was well worn now and the stump below it was deeply cut by Inky's persistent chewing, aided, no doubt, by Pepper, perhaps Salt, and other porky visitors.

We had not long to wait for Inky that night. We heard his little grunt of greeting back in the forest in response to our call. It had been several nights since we had visited him, and perhaps he was just a little bit lonesome. However, he always acted so self-sufficient and utterly indifferent to us that it was difficult to know whether we were very important to him or not.

Now he appeared in the rays of our flashlights, walking along with his head to the ground as if his great load of quills were about all he could carry.

"Inky knows individual responsibility, doesn't he?" said Carol, her own experience still vivid in her thoughts. "Bet he didn't have to get lost to learn it either."

Inky was close to our feet by this time. He took the cookie Carol offered him—although he always had a way of taking such things that made us think he was doing us the favor. He ate a few bites of the delicacy, and then with utter disdain dropped the rest on the ground and stood looking up at us. Carol stooped and stroked his head. He tried to make a playful bite at her hand, but she had learned well how to avoid him.

"I believe he will talk tonight," said Carol, with a wink at me. "He just looks like it."

Yes, Inky looked as if he would talk. Perhaps it is because we know noise is so empty and meaningless that we believe everything silent is made up of deeper wisdom. Inky was doubly silent that night: he did not indulge in his little grunts, and he did not dance. He just sat there looking at us, blinking a bit at the lights, and occasionally scratching an itchy spot with either fore or hind foot. I sat on the ground before him, and he came forward and put his front feet in my lap, and then with a little groan of relaxation he lay down contentedly.

"Is he talking now?" asked Carol, tempting me. "Giny and I can't hear away over here."

"Well," said I, "if you can't hear him, then he is talking."

I looked down in the old porcupine's face, wishing I could give up to repose as easily and as completely as he did.

Inky yawned cavernously, started to scratch back of one ear and then gave it up as too much trouble.

"Sammy, old boy," he seemed to be saying, "I want to add a bit to the things you've been learnin' today."

All right, Inky, go ahead. We'll just skip the question as to how you know we've been learning anything.

"This business of *individual responsibility*"—he paused and looked up to see if I were impressed by his use of such enormous words—"this *individual responsibility* has got a catch to it where you people are concerned. Your job is a bit bigger than ours. We forest people don't have any choice. We just have to obey the law. Every last one of us has got to be the best one he can all the time. We don't know anything else. Same is true of plants or trees. They just have to keep growing their best, and there isn't anything inside of them that says, 'What do you want to do that for? Why should you do everything that is right, when maybe others

won't be doin' their part?' There is where you human
beings are handicapped. You've got a funny ability to
doubt, and to make choices. Most all of you really
know that you ought to live under the same law as the
forest. You would have a mighty swell world if each
one of you would just be the finest fellow you can be.
But there you start doubtin' and questionin'. You think
that is so blamed smart, and yet it's your biggest problem."

"You wouldn't want us to stop reasoning things out,
would you, Inky?" I put in.

"No, I don't mean that." Inky changed his position
and yawned again. "It's good to reason things out. But
you folks don't always reason. You just fear. When
the little old voice of wisdom says inside you, 'You
gotta be the finest human being you can be,' you say,
'Well, OK, but what about the rest of these folks? If I
follow that pattern and the others don't they will take
advantage of me.' And you all go along doin' lots that
is wrong while you believe you would do what is
right if everyone would. Now, Sammy, the world
doesn't work that way. Take that old hemlock tree of
mine, for instance. If it was the only tree in the world,
it would still be the best tree it knows how. If you could
take all the rest of the trees away (and sometimes it
looks as if you people meant to do just that) it wouldn't
get mad, resentful, mean and just quit tryin'. It would
keep on growin' as if the whole world depended upon

it alone. Now that is what you call individ—er—individ——"

"Individual responsibility?" I suggested.

"Thanks," said Inky. "I just wanted to see if you knew."

Inky rose, shook his quills, and looked into the darkness. I knew his moves. Our visit was about over. He raised on his hind legs and reached up with his twitching nose. Carol offered him another cookie, but he wasn't interested. He hadn't quite finished his silent oration.

"Listen, folks," he said, though I am sure Giny and Carol did not hear him, as they were listening to some sound out in the forest: "you people are kind of pathetic. You want to be rid of your troubles, your politics, poverty, wars and such things, and you try one thing after another that doesn't work, when your only way is nature's way. A long time ago Someone said as much to you, and you didn't listen. It was something about doin' your own work, mindin' your own business, or something about salvation——"

"Work out your own salvation," I helped Inky out, "for to this end God worketh with you."

"By Balsam Juice, that's the one! Boy, if you'd only learn to do that, you'd straighten yourselves out in a hurry. We forest folk have known that for ages. Boy, oh boy, it's a swell world when anyone can work out his own starvation."

"Salvation, Inky," I corrected.

"OK, whatever you call it, it's a swell world when everyone can get busy at that business of findin' his own happiness, and that way help others to find theirs. And that reminds me, I didn't do a very good job of chewin' on that cedar tree today. Gotta get busy. So long."

And with sudden animation he went scampering into the forest.

"Wish I had listened more closely," said Carol as I repeated Inky's conversation on the way home. "He has something when he says 'you can be happy in working out your own salvation'—for I had a wonderful time today working out mine!"

XIV

A PORKY AND A *YOUNG PUNK*

Finding the Source of Faith and Strength

THE north wind was still strong, though the rain was over. Little islandlike clouds drifted through the azure sky, and the ruffled lake waters sparkled in the morning sun, as if some spirit were sowing seeds of diamonds.

It was a little difficult to be very cheerful at the breakfast table this morning of Carol's last full day at the Sanctuary. Jokes were pointless, and smiles a bit forced. Carol sat looking distantly out the window while her food grew cold.

And I had a story to tell which only added to her regrets. During the night I had heard something breaking through the brush on the island. Careful not to awaken the others, I had slipped out, flashlight in hand, and discovered a good-sized bear still dripping wet from his swim. He was moving with obvious purpose. The island was only a resting place in a longer journey. There was no time to call Giny and Carol, for when I discovered the creature he was at the point of leaving the island. As he realized he was discovered he emitted the bear's typical *Who-o-o-sh!* and ran to-

227

ward the water, snapping off a good-sized young tree that happened to be in his path. I could see his great black head plainly as he swam away, and long after he had disappeared into the darkness I heard his huge paws occasionally break water.

Carol was ready to feel sorry for herself anyway that morning, and this story of the bear gave her the opportunity. It was bad enough, she thought, that she had to go home the next morning, without missing her only chance to see a bear.

We walked around the island and found the animal's tracks. It was easy to see where he was when he first caught wind of me, for his claws had dug in deeply as he sprang forward. His tracks were plain where he had gone down the bank into the water. And Carol looked long in the direction he had gone as if hoping he might be stuck on a wave and held there. She looked with amazement at the splintered tree the animal had broken off in his flight.

"You would have seen enough of bears if you had been here when Bunny Hunch and Big Boy came," I remarked, recalling with a shake of my head our experience with two pet cubs. "Speaking of nuisances, they made Inky and Salt look like angels."

Many years had passed since these two bears had been at the Sanctuary. Still the region round about wore scratches and scars left by their dynamic activity. Under a tree stood the two crates in which the animals had been shipped to us. The wood was decaying and the heavy wire rusting, but Carol could still see the marks of bear claws and teeth in the heavy boards. Babies though those creatures were at the time, they were already displaying the amazing strength of their kind.

Carol listened to the story of those famous cubs and became almost as excited as if she were seeing them herself.

Never would we forget the day the bears arrived. Giny had not yet become Mrs. Campbell, and my fine friend Bobby was with me at the Sanctuary at the time. Even now in his letters written from far-off military camps, he speaks often of this experience.

We were expecting the bears, for we had agreed to accept them and liberate them in the forest. The two orphaned cubs had been raised by conservation wardens. It was thought that it was time to turn them loose, so that they might make their own way in the world. As they were not in the least frightened by human beings, it would have been unfair to liberate them in hunting territory; therefore, the plan was to let them live under the protection of our Sanctuary.

Remember the fabled Pandora's box, which when opened liberated evils in the world? Well, it was much the same when we opened the two crates in which those sixty-pound cubs arrived. Bobby said he was sure the whole Sanctuary cringed a little when the two creatures climbed out, shook themselves, and started looking around to see where to start their mischief.

The first cub to emerge was whining a little, acting babyish. We tried to call her "Honey Bunch," but stuttered a little in our excitement and said "Bunny Hunch"—and she was Bunny Hunch from then on. The next bear was plainly larger. "Hi there, Big Boy," Bobby called in greeting, and so the team of Bunny Hunch and Big Boy was named.

The bears had had a long train ride and were hungry. We prepared a bite of lunch totaling—before they were through with half a dozen helpings—eight loaves of bread and six quarts of milk!

After this dainty repast, they began a survey of their new surroundings. They were a six-ring circus all rolled up into two black hides. Obviously they were happy in their new surroundings. Until now they had known only a fenced-in pen with a single tree in it. Now here were hundreds of trees, old logs to paw to pieces, bushes, plants, lily pads, lakes—we could almost hear them yell "Who-o-opeee!" as they raced about in their new paradise. They tumbled about like two overgrown puppies, bit and cuffed each other around, tipped over our woodpile, and paused long enough to pull several boards off their crates just to make sure they wouldn't be put in those things again.

"Now we had better train them right from the beginning," Bobby said, though his ambition in this direction was greater than his ability. We might as well have tried to train an earthquake. For the first few hours we didn't know for sure whether it was day or night—all we knew was we had two bear cubs on our hands. Every few minutes either Bobby or I was seeking the other to exclaim excitedly, "Do you know what they have done now?" And then there would be an account of some new depredation they had committed. We had just done the washing, and it was hanging out to dry. Right before our eyes those cubs broke down the line and went racing away in the highest glee, dragging clean clothes all through the brush and over the dirt. We found the line later far down the shore line, dirtier than it had ever been before washing. After they had been quiet for a while, we looked out on the lake to find all our boats adrift. The ropes by which they had been tied had been chewed in two by the bears. And how they loved to play with us—unfortunately! They would race at us, rise on their hind legs and plant their front feet forcefully in our midships. Often this happened when we were not prepared, and Bobby and I took many a sudden seat on the ground.

After the first few hectic hours, their excitement abated somewhat and they settled down to a bit milder living. But we had to remain on the alert. We never knew what was going to happen next.

Certainly their table manners could have been improved. They ate anything and lots of it. When mealtime came they knew it, and sat watching our back door like two black bombs all ready to explode. When we would emerge with the kettle of food (looking like enough to feed a regiment) they would make a run for us that made us feel like the man who catches the kick-off in a football game. Bears are related to pigs, and their family ties are most obvious. They seemed to try to climb right in that kettle—both of them at once. There would be a battle that sounded as if they intended to tear each other to pieces. And we, with never a "please" or "thank you" to pay us for our trouble, would usually be sitting helplessly on the ground, sometimes with the food spilled all over us and the bears gathering it up with their tongues.

Then we learned a little trick. We would open and shut the back door several times to attract their attention. As they watched that door ominously, we would slip out the front door and have their food all placed out in separate pans before they discovered us. But eventually they learned the trick. When we slammed the back door as a decoy, they would race to the front door. When we altered our strategy and tried to come out the back door, one of them stayed at each place. We couldn't win.

There wasn't the usual compensation with these animals. Salt, Inky, Pepper, Rack and Ruin—all had given us the joy of petting them. They liked to be cuddled. Not so with these bears. Only one quieting touch of intimacy did we experience with them. They would stand still while we scratched back of their ears. It seemed to be the spot on their bodies they couldn't scratch themselves, and they accepted our help. But patting or petting—it didn't mean a thing to them. Their pesky hides are so thick, no ordinary sensation gets through.

They were amusing, though, and in spite of our troubles, Bobby and I were nearly sick from laughter. One day when Bobby made a trip to the village for supplies, he brought back some highly colored toy balloons. The cubs had never seen anything like them, and the big babies were frightened to their wits' end. Bobby first let the balloons drift from the back porch to the ground near where the bears were lying sunning themselves. They took one look at these strange objects and with wild snorts raced away into the woods, kicking huge clods of dirt into the air as they went. It was so sudden, so unexpected, and struck us as being so funny that Bobby and I doubled up with that kind of laughter which won't come out. Tears came to our eyes, and we leaned against each other to keep from falling.

But there was more excitement to come! The bears were returning out of the brush, a step at a time, eyes focused nervously on the balloons which were rolling lightly about on the ground. On they came, with hesitant steps and many an inquisitive sniff and threatening growl. Were not they, the bears, kings of the forest?

Did not every living creature stand back when they came near? What were these funny-looking puffed-up colored creatures that dared drift right up to their noses without fear? They approached stiff-legged and tense, as if entering the battle of their lives. The balloons calmly rolled about. At last the bears were within reach

of the balloons. Simultaneously each raised a great paw and struck a blow that would have crumbled a rock. *Pop* went one balloon, *pop* went another—and away went the bears faster than before, kicking clods of dirt high in the air and breaking down every bush that appeared in their paths! Bobby and I leaned against each other again, our faces spread in ghastly grins, tears coursing down our cheeks, but not a sound of laughter coming out.

The bears repeated the stunt time and again, until we couldn't stand it any more. We went in the cabin and sat there until we could really laugh it out. Bunny Hunch and Big Boy never did overcome their fear of those balloons. Probably it was the mystery that impressed them. What could a fellow do when he was facing some sort of creature that just disappeared when he slapped it?

One day when the bears were swimming came the most amusing episode of these balloon experiences. We saw them playing about in the water, and thinking something unusual might happen, we went upwind from them and released several balloons on the water. The light little things drifted rapidly toward the bears. Suddenly the animals discovered them. They actually screamed. Lunging forward with all their power, they went swimming frantically downwind. The balloons, of course, followed them. It was almost too much, and those bears swam as never their kind swam before. They left a wake behind them like that from a launch. Finally they reached a distant shore and raced puffing and half exhausted back into the woods. It was late in the day when they returned, and for once they were quiet. Bobby and I were quiet too, for we had laughed until we were as exhausted as they.

Bobby and I kept up our courage and patience through those summer months with one hope: if we could keep those bears from utterly destroying the

Sanctuary and perhaps ourselves before winter, they would enter hibernation. Probably by spring they would have forgotten us to some extent, and take to life in the forest. But it was a long time until winter, and there was many a problem to come. Nothing was safe or sacred with those bears. They pulled down or pushed over everything that would move, and scratched or bit everything that wouldn't. When the autumn rains set in, we were greeted with a surprise that was far from pleasant. Water started streaming through the roof. An inspection revealed the fact that our pets had been on the cabin roof and pulled off the roofing paper! While we were looking over this calamity and deciding how to fix it, we carelessly left a ladder leaning against the house. Big Boy promptly climbed up on it and poked his paw through a window. They took to sleeping under the cabin, and sometimes in the middle of the night we would be awakened by the wildest snarling and growling as they scuffled with each other. The vocalizations of bears are far from lullabies.

We were happy to see them begin to get sluggish and sleepy as the first cold days came. Surely they were going into hibernation. When we left to give lectures in distant cities, we felt that our problem with Bunny Hunch and Big Boy was at an end. We were entirely too optimistic. Shortly after Christmas time, word reached us that a forester had visited our cabin and the bears were wandering around, looking sleepy but not asleep.

This would not do. If they were up and using the energy of moving about, they had to have food. When a bear hibernates, all bodily activity is reduced to a minimum, so that he can live by absorbing the layers of fat he has stored for the purpose. But if our pets were not sleeping, they needed help. Back we went to the north woods, and with sleds and snowshoes we reached the Sanctuary with a load of food and bales of straw. Bunny Hunch and Big Boy were there all right, walking about as if in a stupor. They took our food, accepted the straw beds we prepared for them, and once more we felt that they were ready to sleep for the winter.

The bears got through the winter all right, but in the spring they did not take to the wildwood as we had hoped. This Sanctuary was a right good boarding-house, and they had no notion of leaving it. Besides, they had become accustomed to human companionship. People were part of their lives, and they did not forget this as we had hoped they would. And it was this fact that led to our next and most embarrassing adventure.

Bobby and I were somewhat delayed in returning to the Sanctuary that following spring. My neighbor—the same one whom Salt chose to annoy—arrived at his cabin first. Bunny Hunch and Big Boy were awake and wandering about our grounds, probably wondering where those human beings could be.

One day there was pounding at my neighbor's cabin,

as he and a hired man began taking down storm windows and opening doors. The bears recognized those sounds as the kind that human beings make, and they went to investigate. They were good-sized bears by this time, and the quarter-mile swim to our neighbors' home meant nothing to them. But imagine the surprise the men experienced when they heard splashing in the water near their pier, and looked down to see two bears emerging and running toward them. Not knowing they were friendly bears, the men ran too. That was wonderful to Bunny Hunch and Big Boy. Not only were human beings coming back, but these men had not forgotten how to play!

After the men they went, the chase leading around and around the house—the men believing they were running for their lives, the bears having a hilarious time. Finally the men ran into the boathouse and slammed the door shut, where they stood puffing, their hearts beating hard after what they believed was a narrow escape from disaster.

The bears looked over the situation a bit. They had seen boathouses before, and knew that there were generally two ways to get into them, one through a door on the land side, and the other through another larger entrance on the lake side. They tried the latter way, and it was open. Splashing and snorting, the bears came swimming in one door, and the men went running out the other.

Now the men climbed into a boat in supposed desperation and pushed out from shore. But when they started to row they found they had only one oar! In the meantime the bears were poised on the shore watching them. Thinking this a part of some new kind of play, they plunged into the water and headed for the boat. It is improbable that one oar has ever propelled a boat faster than happened on that day. The water fairly churned. Fortunately, there was an outboard motor on the boat, and my neighbor succeeded in getting it started. He said the sound of that engine was the sweetest music he ever heard. As the boat skimmed away, the bears followed awhile, and then disappeared into the woods—the men sang hymns of gratitude.

This was the story which greeted us when we arrived at the Sanctuary a few days after our neighbors' exciting adventure. We knew what it meant. We could not have bears and neighbors at the same time. Bunny Hunch and Big Boy then were caught in big boxes and taken away. She went to a park farther in the north woods where she has good care and other bears for companions. He was taken to the state game farm many miles to the south. Big Boy's ride was an epic. He was fairly contented with his box until it was loaded on a trailer and the journey began. Then he decided to break out. He clawed and chewed thick boards to slivers. The men who had him in charge kept nailing new boards on the outside of the crate as he ripped them off on the inside. All the way down the highway this contest continued, and the men arrived at the game farm with their troublesome charge just as their stock of boards and nails was exhausted. Big Boy walked out of his crate calmly, as if nothing had happened, and contentedly took up life in his new home.

"Are bears the strongest animals in the world?" asked Carol, as the story was finished. Her eyes were dancing and her face flushed with merriment.

"That is a difficult question to answer, Carol," I said. "In nature strength is quite a different thing from what we human beings think it."

No doubt the bear can vanquish in combat any other creature in the North American woods. But that is no honest measure of strength. Each creature in nature seems to have the kind of strength and the amount of it needed for his way of living. Proportionately, the bear performs no such feats as the ant, which will lift loads many times its own weight. He will hardly equal the doings of a delicate butterfly, which will flap its frail wings the width of an ocean. There is a power in the things of creation which cannot be measured in terms of muscle and sinew. What is the force which lifts rivers of sap from the roots of trees to the outermost twigs and leaves? What is the power of growth which leads a mushroom to thrust its frail head through crusted soil, pushing aside stones or sticks as it goes? What enables the roots of plants to thread themselves through cracks in solid rocks and finally break them in pieces?

"It fits well with our thought for today that we look into this power of life and growth," I said. "Suppose we go to the old forest-fire area. There is something there that I want to show to you."

Giny, Carol and I paddled our canoe to a point on the lake shore where once had raged a forest fire. Here had stood a marvelous forest of hemlock and pine. In the early days at the Sanctuary we had roamed much in these forest halls. The peace of the ages rested in them. The forest floor beneath the great trees was carpeted thickly with pine needles, softening the footfall of all visiting creatures. This was the "forest primeval." Then came fire—which is the forest's *prime evil*. Someone was careless and burned some brush when a high wind was blowing. Sparks flew far and wide, and before the fire had burned itself out, many miles of beautiful woods lay in smoldering ruin.

Everything seemed destroyed. For years following, the area showed only blackened stumps—a monument to human carelessness. And yet there was one thing that was not destroyed: that is, the principle of growth. That marvelous power which made those woods grow in the beginning would make them grow again. The seed was not lost. Right among the decaying stumps of that old-time forest new trees began coming up. There were balsams, pines, hemlocks—hundreds and thousands of them. They cracked the surface soil, nosed their way through matted leaves and old logs, up through grasses and ferns—up toward the sunlight which was calling them. Human ignorance had presented the forest with a problem, but the trees were equal to it because the power of growth comes from a source that is never defeated and never exhausted!

"And Carol," said I, as we stood among those young virile trees, marveling at the power displayed before us, "it is the same with men and nations. The glorious power which results in good character is never defeated. That which in our better moments makes us rise to the grandeur of rendering service, love, friendship, self-sacrifice and the doing of good works—that cannot be destroyed. There are forest fires of a sort that sweep through our society—wars, epidemics of selfishness and sensualism. Sometimes it seems that our best institutions lie in smoldering ruins like the burning stumps of this forest. But just as these trees rise again through that power we cannot see and cannot stop, so our own civilization lives and rises again, lifted by irresistible spiritual force. Do you see more clearly what is the real strength and force we find in nature? It is not *in* what we see, as much as it is *back* of all that exists."

Carol nodded, but she was too deep in thought for the moment to speak. We walked in silence through the avenues of young trees, touching those nearest us as if we were petting them.

"Do you mind if I talk this out with Inky—this evening?" Carol asked, with a little smile.

"You mean—go to him alone?"

"Yes, please. I won't get lost, I promise."

And that evening Carol went alone to the mainland and down the short trail to the salt lick. Giny and I were much pleased that she wanted to do so. It meant that she had learned to love solitude, and that fear of darkness and silence were no part of her.

She was gone a long time, so long that we walked down to our pier and watched toward the mainland. Presently we saw her flashlight back among the trees as she came down to her boat.

"Did you find Inky?" we asked as she landed on the island.

"Yes, I did."

"And did he talk to you?" Giny and I laughed, but Carol did not.

"It was silly of me ever to think he couldn't," she said. She was ashore now and we three stood looking at the dark mansion where Inky lived. "He looked so quiet and wise," Carol went on, "as if he had inside information on everything. And while I sat looking at him I believe I was more quiet than I have ever been before. Then I learned your secret. Inky talks with silence instead of sound. He speaks in your thoughts.

243

Tonight he spoke in mine—at least I thought he did!"

"Carol, Carol—I guess you *have* learned my secret," I said, laughing delightedly. "Now what do you think he said?"

Carol had found old Inky in very candid mood. Sometimes he was almost rude. It was the first time he had seen her alone, and he wasn't quite sure of her. He came near, then ran away. A few minutes later he returned again, and stood looking inquisitively at her. She tried to pet him, but he raised his quills and acted *tough*. Finally he gained confidence and crawled into her lap, where he sat in his characteristic silence.

Carol stroked Inky's head and fed him a few bites of cookie. She was thinking of the things she had learned that day.

"Some right good ideas you got there, considerin' you're just a young punk," said Inky, according to Carol. "But I wonder if you're smart enough to catch the real point."

"What do you mean, Inky?" Carol had asked.

"Well, you noticed how strength comes to things in nature. That's all well and good. Did you ever watch me climb a tree or bite through a stick? It takes a lot of pep to do that, and I know just how to do it. I have to have faith in that Source of all Power. I have to know that I am taken care of by something that is bigger than I am. But—aw, Balsam Juice, a young punk can't understand things like that."

"Yes, I can, Inky," Carol had insisted. "I know what you mean—please go on."

"Well—I'll try," said Inky skeptically. "It may be a waste of my good north-woods breath, but I'll try. Did you ever hear or read a lesson something about looking at the birds of the air and the lilies of the field?"

"Yes, I know that lesson," said Carol, "and I like it."

"Yes, but you didn't really learn it," snapped Inky, chattering his teeth a bit. "Not many of you folks do learn that. You remember that lesson says to look at these lilies and birds and see how swell they get along in the world. It points out how well they are taken care of—much better than the rich and famous fellows you folks often write about. But the lesson goes on. It says you human beings are even better than they are. Sometimes I think that goes a little too far. I don't see so much that's superior in you people. But never mind that. The lesson says that your Heavenly Father is takin' care of you, givin' you strength and everything you need. And then what does it call you?"

Carol was silent, trying to think out the answer.

"There!" said Inky. "There you are. That's just what I thought. You heard the lesson lots of times, and the most important part you don't know. You're mighty glad to have it tell you you are better than other creatures. That kind of pats you on the back and you like to be flattered. And you like the promise that the great

power back of all things is taking care of you. That's
all OK. But you don't like what the lesson tells you
about what to do, and what it calls you."

"You tell me, Inky," said Carol, now very humble.

"Well, by Balsam Juice, it tells you to quit thinkin'
of yourself, to quit bein' all concerned about what is
goin' to happen tomorrow, how you're goin' to get
clothes to wear and things to eat, because the same
Thing that makes a tree grow, a flower bloom, a bird
fly, and us porkies bosses of the world . . ." Inky paused
a moment and straightened out his quills, giving a
quiet little *ahem*. "That same Thing is lookin' after
you. And then—now listen to this, young punk—and
then it calls you 'Ye of little faith!' There's the thing
you gotta face, and it isn't very complimentary. All these
fine things done for you, and still you don't have much
faith in the One who has done them. That's why you
don't get all the help and blessings that are naturally
yours. You don't have faith in the Creator carin' for
His Creation. At least, not many of you do. Sometimes
there is one of you that's smart enough to have this
faith and quit his worryin' about all the fake strength
folks invent with their imaginations. And when someone does that, he goes places. Your leaders, writers,
thinkers—all your great men—they learned this lesson
and held to it. And why the rest of you go on scrappin',
doubtin', forgettin' the things you know is more than I
can see. Why, hang it all on a cedar tree, faith is all

246

you need to bring out all that strength and power God gave you. Faith kinda plugs you in on universal current. It's the way you hitch yourself up to all the strength you need—if you know what I mean, and I bet you don't."

"But I do know what you mean, Inky," Carol had said. "I learned something about that when I was lost in the woods."

"OK, then, young punk," Inky said with a challenge, "but it's how you live, not what you say that counts. Come back in a year and let me see how you got along, then I'll know if you are smart or not. If you've learned how to work hard and have a good time a-doin' it, if you've learned to treat people decently whether they do as much for you or not, and if you've learned that the faith in that One you folks call your Heavenly Father gives you the strength to do things—mind you, now, I don't say it *does* things for you—it makes you do them *yourself*—then I'll believe in you. But until you prove these things, you're just a young punk. Out of my way now—I got a lotta chewin' to do tonight."

And Inky waddled away unceremoniously, leaving Carol alone with a lot to think about—and to do.

"Carol," I said, as her account was finished, "Inky never spoke in my thoughts any better than he has spoken in yours."

XV

FAREWELL WITH A FUTURE TO IT

ONE October morning the carnival spirit broke loose in the forest. For days trees had been primping and posing, trying on their colorful costumes, getting ready for some gala event. And then came the long awaited hour. That morning the sun was just right—bright and strong. The wind was just right, blowing troops of dancing clouds across a rich blue sky. And as light spread across the world, it revealed the forest multitude in dazzling array. Maples were dressed in rich crimson, oaks in deep maroon, birches wore a golden yellow, sumacs were in startling scarlet, and aspens in vivid orange.

A mood of revelry reigned over the woodland. Everything seemed happy and gay. Surely another event of joy and importance was happening.

An old crow winged his way through the sky, his shrill cry of *caw, caw* echoing on the shores. But to the forest folk it said, "Awake! Awake! the carnival has begun—they are going today, and we must speed them on their way."

"Yes, we are going away today," said Giny, just a bit

sadly, "and the forest celebrates our going just as happily as it did our coming. I am not sure I like that."

But the carnival went on gaining momentarily in hilarity. Red squirrels chattered loudly, ducks darted through the sky, jay birds called, and trees dancing in the breeze pelted us with the confetti of their falling leaves.

Giny and I stood at the shore of our island, our canoe afloat in the shallow water, loaded with baggage. It was time for us to leave our Sanctuary and take up our lecture work in distant cities once more. Emotionally we were in a quandary. We wanted to go, but we wanted to stay. We wanted to reach the thousands of people who would find release from a war-weary world in the nature stories we could bring them. Yet we wanted to watch with our forest friends the coming of winter to our loved north country.

But there was no choice in the matter. The hour had arrived and we were going. We entered our canoe and paddled out into the waters which had been strewn with multicolored leaves. Little waves lapped playfully at the side of our canoe as if goading us along. Giny looked at them somewhat reproachfully.

"This doesn't mean our forest is glad we're going," I said reassuringly. "Nature is just plain glad—no matter what happens. We have to go and so the forest puts on a party. We should be grateful."

"I guess you're right," said Giny, not entirely consoled.

We paddled away slowly, with many a backward look toward our Sanctuary.

Six weeks had passed since Carol had departed. Her going was an exciting though not an entirely joyous event. The woods had crept deeply into her heart, and she did not want to leave. Her baggage was packed at the very last minute, and characteristically she stumbled and nearly fell in the water even as we were entering the boat. Then it was that something happened which sent her away with a laugh in her heart. We had barely enough time to catch her train, when *f-w-e-e-t, f-w-e-e-t* had come the whistle announcing Salt's unwelcome presence at my neighbors' pier. Hurriedly I rowed over to get the pesky porky, while Carol awaited in delight. She petted him a bit and played with him, and with a tear in her voice said good-by. Unsentimental Salt thereupon bit one of the suitcase straps in two, and climbed up a tree.

Several letters from Carol in following days told that she was getting into the swing of things at school. She was remembering what the forest had taught her. "I find I can be quiet in all the confusion," she wrote, "and when I get lost in this excitement I find myself again just the way I did that day near Vanishing Lake."

That is fine, Carol. What you have studied in the woods was not just for use there. Let these things remain in your mind so that they will serve you wherever you are. You have learned what it means to be *quiet*. Never will you need it more than in the hurry and confusion of school and social life. You have seen how nature's children use their play to build their health and prepare them for happy successful lives. If you now choose well your pleasures you will store up treasure for your own future. You have seen what it means to hold a *right attitude,* and what blessings a right sense of *appreciation* can bring. You know how *industry* and *intelligence* serve the children of the forest, and you may prove if you will how they serve you too. And you know the power of *good cheer*. In the lessons of nature you have seen that there is an *individual responsibility* every living thing must assume, and there is no doubt but that you will accept that which is yours. And you saw *strength* that is back of all living things.

Now, child, through your faith keep this strength active in your own life. Sometimes the human world seems in conspiracy against these qualities of nature. Our styles and habits, our aimless way of living, strive to draw us away from such worth-while things. You will be tried, Carol. So-called wise ones will whisper their doubts and in their ignorance attempt to influence you. To all who dare believe in the best comes this test and challenge. But we may hold to our ideals if we will, and thus carve for ourselves lives of accomplishment, usefulness and happiness. Keep those things you have learned at the Sanctuary, for they are real and true!

Giny and I paddled close in to the mainland as we headed out on our winter journey. Back in those groves somewhere lived old Inky—Inky the philosopher, Inky the solitary and saucy porcupine!

My last visit with him had been just the night before. "So you're headin' out, are you, Sammy, old kid?" he had said. "Well, I kinda hate to see you go. You don't know much, but you're willin' to learn. You might give those folks down there a message from me. Tell them to try bein' natural. Yes—just try bein' natural. That's all they need. They get so blamed messed up in their struttin' and pretendin' and there just isn't any good in it. Did you ever think what it means to be natural?"

"Well, I have thought some," I said hesitantly.

"Not very much, I'll bet!" Inky had said with a disapproving little grunt. "Listen—what's the biggest compliment you can give anyone? Let me tell you: it is to say that he is perfectly natural. You know right well, when you say that you mean whoever you are talking about is all right. If he's natural, he's dependable. He says what he means and means what he says. He doesn't bluff and he doesn't lie, for that isn't natural. A perfectly natural person doesn't pat you on the back in front of your face and slap your face behind your back. No sirree! It isn't only what is natural in the forest that is good and beautiful, it's what is natural everywhere—

and I hate to tell you so, but there isn't anything more beautiful than what is natural in you human beings. Now take Carol for instance——"

"You kinda fell for her, didn't you, Inky?" I asked, teasing.

"Aw! Balsam Juice!" said Inky, blushing a bit. "She's OK, I guess. That is if she stays natural, but if she starts a-puttin' on airs and actin' like someone she isn't, she'll lose more than half her charm. And by the way, not that it makes any difference, but er—ah—I mean, she'll be comin' back again, won't she?"

Yes, Inky, Carol will be coming back again. And when she does she will still be as natural and lovable as she was on this first visit.

We paddled on, saying little as the forest festival continued. Tiny shore-line bushes looked out at us and smiled colorfully. Wild asters waved a cheery greeting.

Now we were passing our neighbors' pier. The cabin was boarded up against the coming winter, and our friends had long since left for the sunny South. We smiled as we looked at the pier where Salt had come so often for his ferry service. But we felt sure he would not come again. For two weeks he had been gone now, not even returning to tell us good-by or to take part in our farewell party. Salt and Pepper were together once more! We had come upon them in the forest, heard their little play talk as when they were babies on the island, and found them tussling and wrestling about.

Just when this reunion had taken place we could not know. Perhaps in all of Salt's trips to the mainland he had been visiting his companion. Again, it might be that they had just found each other. At any rate, we had seen them together, played with them, and then watched them race away into the woods in most obvious happiness. This reunion was what we had hoped for, and now that they were together we did not regret leaving them in the forest.

Autumn evenings had brought us many adventures. We felt sure we had seen Bobette at the salt lick on several occasions. At least it was a beautiful doe we saw, and no one could prove it wasn't she. Then once in twilight when we were hiking down a little trail we had seen the Antlered King at the top of a knoll, silhouetted against an evening sky. His antlers were fully grown. No doubt he had been rubbing them against a cedar tree or a balsam, and they were free of the velvet or soft skin which covered them when they were growing. He stood motionless for just a moment. Then with precise step, head held high, ears turning this way and that seeking sounds, he moved away into the forest. And we breathed a prayer into the solitude that he might escape all dangers and live on for us to see again.

The beavers of Beaver Bay were working incessantly. Their house was huge now, and it looked strong enough to withstand an earthquake. Often as we paddled along those shores at night we had heard them at work cutting trees, and always before we had left their realm one or more of them would give the beaver warning of a tail slap and a dive.

Many birds had already left the north country. Purple martins had long since departed to winter in the far south, perhaps even in Venezuela or Brazil. White-throated sparrows had gone, murmuring remnants of

their summer songs, to live in the sunshine of Florida and southern Texas. Our little phoebe had left her nest in the boathouse and flown south, perhaps to Cuba or Mexico. The oven bird, whose call dominates the forest with a shrill *teacher, teacher, teacher, teacher* was well on her way to some southern haunt, perhaps an island in the Caribbean Sea. The blue herons were gone, now to stand still on their stiltlike legs in the swamps of Louisiana or the everglades of Florida.

And yet the woods were not stripped of bird life. As we paddled our canoe through the channel into the next lake, where a car would be waiting for us, a flock of chickadees darted through the foliage of near-by trees. They were gossiping merrily, and no winter blast could frighten them into leaving their beloved northern forests. A wave of gold finches darted across from one shore to the other, their brilliant plumage rivaling the autumn leaves. Back in the woods we could hear a woodpecker drumming rhythmically on an old dead tree.

"We are leaving the Sanctuary in very good shape this year," Giny was saying as we neared our landing place. "All our forest friends seem so well prepared for the winter: Inky is contented, Salt and Pepper are together, the raccoons are happy. It makes going away easier when we know this."

"Yes," I agreed, "I have more comfort now than I had all summer. When we return in the spring, these animals will have taken to the woods and will be independent of us. We will see them, but there won't be any more crunching on our cabin, and no more whistles in the middle of the night. The pestering days of those fellows are over, and I am glad for a little rest."

I was thinking of the many problems our porky pals

had given us during the summer. Giny smiled wisely.

"And another thing," I said with emphasis: "I believe next spring I am not going to accept any more animals to raise, no matter what they are. It would be fine to have time just to read and write and rest for a season, without bears or porkies to worry about. Yes, I have decided! In the springtime I'll watch for our old friends in the woods, but absolutely no new pet animals!"

Just at the moment there was an outburst of the wildest sort of laughter close over our heads.

"Wha! Ha, ha, ha, ha, haw, haw, haw!" An old loon, flying south, had paused to spill his merriment over us. He lighted on the lake where he flapped wildly about, continuing his laughter as if he simply couldn't control himself. Then there was another laugh in higher pitch.

"He, he, he, he," giggled a kingfisher as he dived playfully into the water, and rose to a branch where he could look down at us.

Then a squirrel chattered, as if to say, "Aw! Look who's talkin'. Ha, ha, ha!" And the crows and ravens ovearhead echoed, *"Haw, haw."*

By this time Giny was laughing too. "You see what they think of your resolve," she said, as we were climbing out at the landing. "And anyway, you know better yourself. In the spring you will take any kind of a creature that needs help—from a baby mosquito to an elephant. And the more trouble it is, the better you will like it."

"Well . . ." said I, hesitating to admit what I knew as true. "At least I think next spring can't bring any greater trouble than we have already had."

But it did!—in a very unexpected and original way.